Everyday MOMents

"*Everyday MOMents* is a book filled with advice that will lift your spirit and encourage your heart. The spiritual applications and messages from the scriptures are simple enough to grasp onto in the midst of ordinary routine and will add holy moments into the role of motherhood."
—Emily Belle Freeman, bestselling author
and mother to many children

"In the midst of soaking in Jessica Poe's mothering purity and perspective, I recognized that she was offering me a return to real motherhood. Motherhood through all human history was an apprenticed trait, taught at the feet of generations of mothers, aunts, grandmothers, and sisters all under the same roof. To spend a day under the same roof with a mother such as Jessica Poe is like receiving master training and a return to what this job is all about—*moments* of divinity. Jessica offers countless ways to see motherhood the way God sees motherhood and to create *moments* that God wants and needs us to create for His precious children. Thank you, Jessica, for whispering truths in my head that echo to me through my daily mom routine. The greatest gift will be the day that your thoughts and ideas have become such a part of me that I think your thoughts all on my own and recognize all the *moments* that God gives me."
—Sandra Turley, Time Out for Women
and Broadway singer and mother of four

"This must-read will enlighten every woman in the trenches of motherhood! It's an empowering narrative of 'aha' moments transforming the mundane to the momentous. Readers will instantly find a connection and solidarity with women everywhere—and with heaven above. It's an absolute balm of Gilead for the soul; I'm gifting this to mothers of all ages and stages!"
—Dalee MacDonald, mother of five

Everyday MOMents

Discovering Christ in the Details of Motherhood

Everyday MOMents

Jessica Poe

CFI
An imprint of Cedar Fort, Inc.
Springville, UT

This is not an official publication of The Church of Jesus Christ of Latter-day Saints. The
opinions and views expressed herein belong solely to the author and do not necessarily represent the opinions or views of Cedar Fort, Inc. Permission for the use of sources, graphics,
and photos is also solely the responsibility of the author.

ISBN 13: 978-1-4621-1774-1

Published by CFI, an imprint of Cedar Fort, Inc.
2373 W. 700 S., Springville, UT 84663
Distributed by Cedar Fort, Inc., www.cedarfort.com

Library of Congress Cataloging-in-Publication Data

Names: Poe, Jessica, 1980- author.
Title: Everyday MOMents : discovering Christ in the details of motherhood /
  Jessica Poe.
Description: Springville, Utah : CFI, an imprint of Cedar Fort, Inc., [2016]
  | "2016 | Includes bibliographical references.
Identifiers: LCCN 2015038454 | ISBN 9781462117741 (perfect bound : alk. paper)
Subjects: LCSH: Motherhood--Religious aspects--Church of Jesus Christ of
  Latter-day Saints. | Church of Jesus Christ of Latter-day
  Saints--Doctrines. | Mormon Church--Doctrines.
Classification: LCC BX8643.W66 P635 2016 | DDC 248.8/431--dc23
LC record available at http://lccn.loc.gov/2015038454

Cover design by Shawnda T. Craig
Cover design © 2016 Cedar Fort, Inc.
Edited and typeset by Jessica B. Ellingson

Printed in the United States of America

10 9 8 7 6 5 4 3 2 1

Printed on acid-free paper

There is a spiritual meaning of all human acts and earthly events. . . . It is the business of man to find the spiritual meaning of earthly things. . . . No man is quite so happy . . . as he who backs all his labors by such a spiritual interpretation and understanding of the acts of his life.
(John A. Widtsoe, in Conference Report, April 1922, 96–97)

For my sweet children, who gave me the eternal role of mother. You teach me more than I could ever teach you, and you bring indescribable light and joy to my life.

For my forever husband, who allows me to be the mother of his children and who generously offers support, friendship, encouragement, and time to write. Oh, how I love you.

For my faith-filled mother, who dedicates so much of her life to improving mine. Thank you for believing in me more than I believe in myself. You are an angel, a rock, and a role model.

For my earthly father and my Heavenly Father, who provide life, love, and examples to strive for. Thank you for your eternal love and presence.

Contents

Introduction

A mother's role is sacred, a duty of divine design. I've heard it before. I know it's true. Yet I easily lose sight of my spiritual significance while I'm actually doing it— you know, being a mother. The message about mothers and their importance is out there (though sometimes brushed aside). I'm thankful for the message, as it has always rung true to my soul. In fact, I believe in that message so strongly that I chose to devote my adult life to motherhood. I know both the responsibilities and blessings are great because of this choice, and I can't think of anything more honorable than being in a partnership with my Heavenly Father and husband in rearing these beautiful children. Yet even with this knowledge, my precious testimony of the sacred and extremely spiritual role of being a mother gets stuffed to the rear of my mind—when it needs to be centered in the forefront.

I wonder if I'm the only mother who feels that way. I stare in awe at the heroic veteran mother hens in my congregation. They carefully gather their fluffy-feathered chicks and guide them down chapel aisles while balancing diaper bags, Sunday School lesson plans, quiet books—all in high heels. It's as if they know just how to gracefully lead their long train of posterity toward eternity. I wonder if from sunup to sundown they warmly nurture every chirping chick on their family farm without losing sight of the divine mission they possess.

On the other hand, my family farm feels more like a funny farm. Somewhere between the nose-pinching dirty diapers, the

1

power struggles, the always-hungry stomachs, and the constant losing battle with dirt, the spiritually idealistic mommy moments (*moments*) become as unrealistic as reverence for an entire Church service.

Let's look back to that Church service again. As I envision those mother hens amongst the congregation, looking impressively flawless in their Sunday best, I must remember that I really know these women. We're all connected in the web of womanhood, our children play together, and we collaboratively rear our children. I know one mom struggles with potty-training her five-year-old, another is newly remarried and in the thick of blending two families, one worries about her husband's impending job loss, a dear friend yearns for children of her own, and another feels like she's barely surviving as she snuggles twin baby girls and a toddler recovering from leukemia. The reality is that while these moms are super, they're not untouchable superheroes. Super Moms don't exist.

Every mother experiences years in the trenches, armed with wipes and willpower. Every mother knows sleepless nights, heartaches and headaches, antibiotics and anti-aging creams, sacrifice and service, laughter and losing oneself, and love. Even composed mothers who appear on top of their game—yes, even the most veteran, the most put-together mother hens—need frequent reassurance of their big-picture duties.

Too often the daily goo and sticky fingerprints muck up my mind so I'm not seeing the spiritual side of my mothering life. I'm learning to rely on a heaven-sent technique that has proven to remove worldly residue and clear up the view of my life's divine purpose. It's all about seeking symbols and His sight while experiencing the everyday mommy moments. It's about opening my sleep-deprived eyes to see what He's trying to teach me. I've found that the skill can turn the most ordinary and tiresome moments into extraordinary teaching *moments*. It's a skill and a process I'm constantly practicing and fine-tuning, but it's making me a better mother, teacher, friend, and person. And in my wildest dreams, that small idea catches fire and spreads to help my fellow mothers too.

Please note: This book is intended for believers in the Lord Jesus Christ, regardless of religious denomination. As a member of The Church of Jesus Christ of Latter-day Saints, I believe the Book of Mormon to be a revealed witness of Jesus Christ that goes hand-in-hand with the Holy Bible. Thus, I include references from both the Holy Bible and the Book of Mormon in my writings. That said, any mothering hearts who seek to come closer to Christ can benefit from reading and practicing the principles in this book. Thank you for your openness, acceptance, and support.

CHAPTER 1

Wake-Up Call

6:00 a.m.

Sunrays creep over the horizon and through my horizontal blinds. My mind debates between springing to life and hibernating through at least one more snooze session. My eyes remain closed while I picture the dewdrops pooling in pockets, waiting for absorption, and hear the tree swallows swooping through the sky, chirping of chances. It seems Mother Nature's cues call for one thing today: possibilities.

So, when my husband uncurls my cocoon of blankets to give me a peck as he rushes out the door for his daily commute downtown, I decide to give the day—and him—a worthy send off. His freshly sprayed cologne acts as my smelling salt, waking my senses enough for me to croak an "I love you" after our sweet smooch. He lingers, and his smoothly shaven cheek rests on mine. He's not even scared away by my monstrous morning breath—ah, true love. He's my favorite way to start the day.

Though I dream of falling back to sleep in his safe embrace, I know what's coming. Three little voices will soon call my name, and six little hands will need constant help.

Unlike me, those little ones wake up with instant energy. "Get up and go" takes on a whole new meaning as they catapult into their day with boundless energy. Amazingly, even at night, they

5

continue to wind up instead of winding down. To match their vigor and vim, I need a miracle—every day!

That's why I wake up a wee bit earlier than them. I reserve a precious one-hour jumpstart, and it immediately comes with tough decisions. Will I read scriptures, exercise, write (either in my journal or for work), shower, or power up the computer? Usually I aim for a value-pack combination.

Like a good girl, I pick up my scriptures first. I've found that when I kick off my day with scriptures, I accomplish much more than when I don't. (Okay, I do recognize my selfish motive behind scripture study—kind of pathetic but totally honest.)

For some time, I've been reading the words of our prophets with a particular quest in mind. During the daily tornado of life with little ones, I often find myself stuck in survival mode. I seem to be treading water in the sea of whines, barely breathing beneath the messes of mass destruction and constantly redirecting the fiery darts of my little brood's feuds. Throughout the boot camp and battles, my precious testimony of the sacred and extremely spiritual role of mother gets stuffed to the rear of my mind when it needs to be in the forefront. So I ask myself and the Lord, "How can I see the extraordinary spiritual side of my ordinary, everyday life?"

I flip open my Bible and come to Genesis 28, when Isaac sends Jacob on a journey to find a wife. After traveling all day, Jacob rests, and during his sleep he experiences an unforgettable dream. He sees the Lord and hears Him speak. Christ promises Jacob seed as numerous as the dust of the earth and promises that through him and his seed, all the families of the earth will be blessed.

Then the sixteenth verse pops out to me: "And Jacob awaked out of his sleep, and he said, Surely the Lord is in this place; and I knew it not."

I know the Lord is in this place—in my house and especially in my role as mother—but I can't seem to awaken out of my sleep-deprived state to see it. How can I shake off the sleep blocking my spiritual eyes and see the Lord in my day-to-day?

"As we are spiritually awake and alert, we see His hand across the world and we see His hand in our own personal lives," said

Elder Neil L. Anderson ("Thy Kingdom Come," *Ensign*, May 2015, 120). That's exactly what I want—to be spiritually awake and alert to His hand.

My mind flashes back to a seminary lesson—an unusual occurrence. I don't reminisce about seminary lessons often—even though I loved and craved seminary in my high school years. My family and I joined The Church of Jesus Christ of Latter-day Saints a few months prior to high school registration, and as a fresh convert soaking up the gospel, I loved seminary and devoured every principle.

I picture gray-suited Brother Rasmussen in front of our class, reading a scripture mastery verse in Isaiah and telling us that God's lessons can be found in anything. *Anything.* The absoluteness of his message struck me, or perhaps it was the Spirit. Either way, I knew it was important enough to remember.

Breaking out of another blanket layer, I thumb to Isaiah in the same scripture set I used for seminary and find the faded scripture mastery markings, decades old but still flagging the right place: "For my thoughts are not your thoughts, neither are your ways my ways, saith the Lord. For as the heavens are higher than the earth, so are my ways higher than your ways, and my thoughts than your thoughts" (Isaiah 55:8–9).

I grin as I remember my seminary teacher trying to teach a class of immature high school students to ditch the natural man's self-centered thoughts and replace them with Heavenly Father's divine and selfless ones. Brother Rasmussen implored us to replace our view of the details of our life with views from the highest altitude and the most eternal perspective.

There is my answer. To find the extraordinary spiritual side of my ordinary life, I have to swap my thoughts with His.

If spirituality can be found in anything, it can be found in my sometimes mundane and monotonous daily life.

With a newfound goal in mind, I kneel down in prayer to my Heavenly Father. I ask for His insight. I plead to see my daily life as He would have me see it—with spiritual meaning and personalized lessons behind every chore on my to-do list.

After all, the Lord promises, "He who hath faith to see shall see" (D&C 42:49).

With faith that I'll be blessed to see my moments as He would have me see them, I decide to write down my experiences. President Henry B. Eyring gave an address that still clings to my soul about preserving our spiritual experiences. During that talk, he shared what the Spirit once said to him: "I'm not giving you these experiences for yourself. Write them down" ("O Remember, Remember," *Ensign*, November 2007, 66).

By acknowledging and responding to spiritual promptings, we show gratitude for the Holy Ghost's instructions, and by permanently recording those promptings, we can be blessed with remembering our insights. Trust me, these days I need all the help I can get with remembering things!

I select a small spiral notebook and pen my quest at the top: Seeing the Divine Details in My Everyday Life.

With this morning's inspiration, I determine to start my experiment immediately. Better now than never, right? Who knows, this could be the beginning of something extraordinary.

YOUR TURN!

Want to play too? Here's how:
1. Grab a notebook.
2. Pray for His sight.
3. With an open mind and heart, look deep; it may take time, but it will come.
4. Continue reading and consider personal application as you go.

Make it a game. I've discovered a surefire and pleasant way to persuade reluctant toddlers to listen and obey when they'd rather wander and play. It's easy. Just reinstate tasks with a game that capitalizes on their newly gifted physical bodies. Tots are eager to figure out all the things their new physical bodies can do. In fact, they love exerting themselves physically so much that they might not even realize they're completing the task (and doing exactly what their mama wants). That's why I'm marching up the stairs like a penguin on parade, slam dunking dirty laundry into the basketball hamper, and stretching in a yoga-styled round of Simon Says to calm rambunctious energy.

Divine details: Apparently I'm the toddler today. Heavenly Father has lessons to teach me, and He has introduced a new game to my mind in attempts to persuade me to listen and obey instead of just wander and play. I think I'll call it Seeking Symbols or Discovering Divine Details. No matter the name of the game, the objective is to locate divine details and insight hidden within ordinary moments filling my ordinary mom day. Heavenly Father knows I'm His kid at heart and will enthusiastically take the bait. It's going be fun.

"Virtually any experience can provide you with just the example, enrichment, or clarification you need for a gospel lesson" ("Lesson 10: Looking for Lessons Everywhere," *Teaching, No Greater Call: A Resource Guide for Gospel Teaching* [Salt Lake City: The Church of Jesus Christ of Latter-day Saints, 1999], 30).

CHAPTER 2

A Personal Symbol

7:00 a.m.

While I lay in bed, half awake, I think of my snoozing crew in dreamy land, little chests moving up and down. My family is young and just taking off—which feels simultaneously exciting and daunting, fleeting and never-ending. So far, I'm helping raise one feminine, imaginative, and intelligent six-year-old girl named Avery; one strong-willed and snuggly four-year-old girl named Anna; and one extroverted all-star, fourteen-month-old boy named Eli. They are my joy, they are my worry, and they are my life. But because I already feel buried in daily temporal responsibilities, I'm losing sight of the sacredness of my spiritual responsibilities.

Stumbling into the bathroom, I switch on the light and shock my system with a splash of cold water. Not wanting to disturb my sleeping beauties in the adjacent room, my fingers tiptoe like ballerinas around the packed drawer, searching for spectacles. Fumbling a bit, I find them and groggily gaze at the mirror. Dark circles frame my eyes, which appear much too old for my face. Dressed in an oversized T-shirt and maternity sweatpants (I'm not pregnant; they're just *so* comfortable), I think to myself, "Is this really me?" The image in the mirror sure doesn't look like what I feel like inside.

What happened to the sun-kissed, glowing bride of my wedding day? All I see now are flaring nostrils, adult acne, and a compressed chest. Perhaps I should invest more currency in the multi-billion-dollar beauty industry. High-quality concealers, skin serums, spray tans, squeezing body shapers, hair highlights, and an upgraded bra could possibly do the trick. With their help, I'd surely look like my youthful self again, right?

I pause my meandering makeover mind to realign with the newfound goal of seeing the divine details and spiritual symbols in my life. Lotions and potions, makeup and fake-up, all add layers to the natural self. That's how the world works. But I'm not seeking to see the world's way; I'm seeking Heavenly Father's way. So instead of adding to cover, maybe I need to peel back and uncover.

I push my nose as close as possible to the mirror, standing face-to-face with myself. The up-close stare-down feels intimidating, as every pore and flaw appears magnified. But that's when I realize these checklists of imperfections place layers of labels on myself, causing me to speak in self-destructive conclusions. I know Heavenly Father sees a much deeper, truer me.

So, I pull back the harsh layers and labels I adhere to myself. I strip away "worn out mom," "weirdo," "not attractive enough," and "not good enough." What's left underneath? What are the words Heavenly Father uses to describe me, since He, my Creator, knows me best?

Thinking back to His personalized words spoken in previous priesthood blessings, two specific words stand out to me: *sweet* and *anchor*. In priesthood blessings, Heavenly Father consistently describes me as sweet, and He admonishes me to remain pure and true to the sweetness within. I look in the mirror and say it out loud, "I'm sweet." I can't help but smile when I say it. Since I'm sweet on sugar, I delight in the word, but more important, I feel like it fits my true personality and spirit.

As for anchor, that precious word has also been used repetitively in priesthood blessings—sometimes as a noun telling me what to become, and sometimes as a verb instructing me about what to do. Though the word typically describes a heavy metal object that secures a vessel in place, when Heavenly Father describes me as an anchor, He's using the very lesson He's trying to teach me: symbolism. He knows that as I anchor myself in Christ, I can be as firmly fixed in the gospel as an anchor is amid swirling storms. This means Heavenly Father thinks of me as reliable, steady, and dependable. He trusts me! It feels amazing to be trusted by God—or at least trusted by God if I live up to my potential. That is an empowering description and label to cling to and strive for. Plus, I love that it is an object—a symbol in itself.

To combine my two heaven-sent labels, I conclude that my ultimate personal symbol should be a sprinkle-covered anchor. I envision pops of bright color, like a colorful cupcake-topper anchor (versus the traditional nautical-style ones). When I think of myself as a sweet, sprinkle-covered anchor and of all the meaning within that symbol, it's hard to contain the delicious glee within. I desire to live up to those words, and I feel a renewed sense of self—my true self.

I'm not the only one with a personal symbol. One of my heroes, and former Young Women president for the Church, Elaine S. Dalton selected her symbol when she was a teenager in the Young Women program.

> My Young Women leaders had each of us choose a symbol that would represent the life that we would live and what we would strive to become as daughters of God. We then stitched these symbols onto our bandlos—which were fabric sashes that we wore. These bandlos were our personal banners to the world! I chose the symbol of a white rose because roses become more and more beautiful as they grow and blossom, and I chose the color white for purity. I encourage each of you to ponder what your personal banner [symbol] would be if you could give one message to the world. (Elaine S. Dalton, "Come Let Us Go Up to the Mountain of the Lord," *Ensign*, May 2009, 121–22)

My fellow homeschooler, an inspiring friend, and a talented artist, Pamela Susan, also has a personal symbol: the honeybee. Not only does her name, Pamela, mean "all honey," but her colorful home is as busy as the beehives in her backyard. Passionately fascinated with bee life, Pam spends significant time learning and teaching about these organized, collaborative, and driven insects.

For example, she taught me about the life stages female worker bees pass through: house cleaning, nursing, wax making, guarding, and foraging. Each bee in each stage has a specific role significant to the colony. And though each stage is different, it comes with great beauty. Likewise, Pam aspires to see and "bee" beauty in each stage of her life.

She also taught me that a queen bee egg starts just the same as a worker bee egg. Here's the catch: the egg that's fed the prized nutrition-packed royal jelly develops into the largest and longest-living bee—the queen. With that in mind, Pam feeds her spirit with the most nutritious and prized royal substance available (the sweet word of God), as she strives to reach her potential of becoming a queen on high.

Personalized symbols bring eternal hope and identity. They're energizing, therapeutic, and inspiring. Flipping open the spiral notebook, I scribble my first finding: "You are the sprinkle-covered anchor."

I head back to my cluttered bathroom counter and think of my husband. It's hard not to think of him when his tracks are so obviously left behind. Scanning the room, I can tell which drawer he was last in (the one left gaping wide open) and which towel he used to dry his hands as he sped out the door. The whiskers stuck to the shower wall testify that his face is clean-shaven, and the toothpaste streaked down the sink swears he brushed his teeth. My husband rises when the moon's still shimmering to prepare for his long commute and even longer day at work. I'm thankful for his dedication and sacrifice to provide for our family—but I cringe at the residue of his morning routine.

The truth of the matter is that we have different visions of clean. My ideal version involves disinfectants, sponges, elbow grease, and even a tiny toothbrush for the sole purpose of scrubbing the shower door tracks. Note: this is the ideal, not a consistent reality. To convince my husband to catch my vision, maybe I should take a picture of the bathroom when it is sparkling and then post the image on the mirror and label it, "The room should look like this when you're finished." It could be a vision statement for cleanliness (especially since vision statements describe potential, not current condition).

I have full confidence in the power of vision statements and have seen them inspire and improve both secular and spiritual entities. After attending a local homeschooling conference, I created a vision statement for our educational pursuits. It actually is posted on my bathroom mirror, and I read it most mornings. The words help my thoughts and spirit align and point me in the right direction for the day. It reads:

> In our home and school life, the heart and core of an individual comes first. In other words, character precedes academics. Our home is full of laughter, deep breaths, music, whimsical moments, work, meditation, service, virtue, books, nature, and love. We seek after the Holy Spirit's constant guidance and look forward with an eternal perspective, trusting that days and years of tiny, ordinary moments, decisions, and habits will transform into deep, royal character and powerful testimonies of Christ. No matter the stage or season, we cherish it. Therefore, we begin each new day and season knowing we received full joy from the last.

Reading it now, I realize how little my homeschool statement says about education. There's not a mention of reading, writing, or arithmetic, let alone science experiments, research reports, dramatic historical reenactments, or field trips. I guess those items didn't make the cut because they're not what I need to focus on. Instead, the vision statement is full of my weaknesses. By instructing me on what to aim for, the vision statement speaks peace to my soul when I worry or doubt; it focuses my mind on the individual brushstrokes that will someday create a glorious eternal masterpiece.

Maybe that's why Heavenly Father wants me to remember and cling to those words *sweet* and *anchor*. My personal symbol is just as much something to strive for as it is a label for my current spiritual condition. I take my notebook and edit the wording slightly. Instead of reading, "You are the sprinkle-covered anchor," it now says, "Be the sprinkle-covered anchor."

Be is a powerful action word, and the gospel is all about action and becoming. As my eyes open to spiritual lessons—whether from looking in the mirror or any other ordinary moment—I must remind myself to apply the lessons as well to become more like Christ. In the Book of Mormon, we are commanded to "liken [the scriptures] unto [ourselves]" (1 Nephi 19:24). Likewise, I can liken my days and *mom*ents unto myself.

From the first glance in the mirror, it appears that my first lesson is to see myself as He would see me. I received the message, and now I need to do something about it. So I take one more look in the mirror. I melt away the focus on hardened lines around my eyes and other physical imperfections and mentally add a white angelic glow. I try to unveil the sweet and anchored heroine within. I count my blessings and talents. I think about character traits I've passed on to my children and how beautiful those traits make them—which means I too am beautiful. I gaze inside and ahead and discover a more divine woman. Not only do I see a wise soul full of faith and trust, but I also feel loved and full of love. I feel inspired and motivated. I feel ready and real. I feel more like the *real* me.

Let the day begin.

YOUR TURN!

Do you have a personal symbol? Would you like to discover one? Look to scriptures, hymns, or words from prophets that have guided crucial decisions in your life and reread your patriarchal blessing and journal entries. Take time to think about who you are now and who you'd like to become. Identify characteristics or symbols you relate to, feel passionate about, and aspire to. With your studies and pondering, be sure to pray. The Lord will lead you to inspiring answers.

The blow-dry. It takes approximately eight minutes to blow-dry my hair, and it's worth every minute. I realize blow-drying one's hair is just a simple process to quicken what will naturally occur anyway, but I've learned that a quality blow-dry increases volume and style and allows for greater control over the outcome of my hair. Plus, if I can withstand the uncomfortable heat and keep that heavy blow dryer lifted until my locks lack any moisture, then that thorough blow-dry can last for days.

Spiritual translation: My physical body will change from young to old no matter what, and I will eventually leave this mortal life. It's just a naturally occurring process that can't be fought. In this example, the hair symbolizes the soul within the body. Heavenly Father heats things up for our spirits by sending experiences and trials. These learning opportunities style our souls, smooth out kinks, curl under split ends, and add volume to our talents. As our master stylist, Heavenly Father has a vision for the glorious outcome. If I can just absorb the heat by enduring to the end, allowing trials to teach my soul the intended lessons, I can maintain His glorious style for me for eternity.

CHAPTER 3

Routines on Repeat

8:00 a.m.

"Mom!"

"Mama!"

"Mom-eeeeee!"

I can hear the distinct trio of voices shouting morning salutes to the queen of the house. When one wakes, the others immediately awaken and sound calls of my divine title.

It's official: the routine starts now.

While Avery and Anna dress in matching hot pink leggings and tutus, Eli rolls his mini basketball between my legs toward the pile of books on the floor. I sing our cheesy good-morning song to them, dump a load of clean laundry on my bed, and begin the monotonous task of folding whites until the grumbling tummies can't last another second without their daily breakfast of muffins and bananas.

Even while I force a good-morning grin, my mind speeds in a million directions. Luckily, the chore at hand requires little to no brainpower. I'm guessing every mom folds clothes—warm from the dryer or leftover strays—on a daily basis. It's not a task I dread, but I don't look forward to it either. It's just a small part of my job description that takes a few minutes each day—like refereeing squabbles, scrubbing wee hands, and scooting the tricycle up the driveway.

Honestly, I feel like the majority of my daily grind repeats itself in twenty-four–hour increments (or sooner). I cook, serve, and clean up meals a minimum of three times a day. I buckle little bodies into car seats, drive the same roads to and from town, pick up the same scattered toys, recite the same beloved stories, and change constantly dirty diapers. In fact, I'd go as far as predicting that 80 percent of today's tasks will be instant replay for tomorrow.

I can't help but ask myself, what spiritual insights can be found from the rhythm of my domestic routine? And why does Heavenly Father want me doing the same mundane dance over and over again?

A few days ago, I chatted with a long-time family friend who lives in Bountiful, Utah. She's in a different chapter of life than I am; her youngest is a senior in high school, and half of her children are married and have completed college. Now she's frantically calculating costs to get the other half finished—you know, returned missionaries clutching college degrees in one hand and an eternal spouse in the other. She explained her worries, threw up her arms, and said, "I'm tired! I've done this several times already, and I want to be done with this phase!"

A few days before that, I gabbed on the phone with my best friend in Boise, Idaho. She's potty training her third daughter, has her fourth in diapers, and has one baking in her maternal oven. She said she was tired too. She just wants to be done with this taxing training phase. She cringed at the thought of potty training again and again.

It seems like no matter what stage we're in, no matter what trials we're going through, repetition remains—making us all very tired!

Grabbing one of my husband's white dress shirts, I grumble out of frustration with myself. The dryer's tumbling rounds stopped hours ago, and I left the clothes all night. Now my husband's shirt doesn't look fresh and pressed but crinkled and wrinkled, like the mouth of an old man scrunched in thought during a church sermon—which leads my meandering mind to my old man.

From the outside, my dad appears to be in the perfect form of handsome health. Inside, however, his body battles cancer—and it's a battle that's been going on much longer than we've known. He's undergone several surgeries and various forms of treatments. Each tactic comes slightly different in technique, but the overall goal remains: kill cancerous cells. Maybe the explanation to our repetitive lifestyle lies in that idea.

Our days, phases, and trials may differ slightly during their repetitive spin cycles, but our overall goal remains solid. My goal is to get through it (whatever "it" may be) a little more like the Savior would. Whether I'm having another routine day or facing a defining moment, I hope to improve my behavior by bettering my thoughts, attitudes, and actions. I'm extremely thankful to know and recognize that goal! If I didn't have an eternal perspective, I'd feel like these droning reruns were part of a muddled and warped plot to tease and annoy. Unfortunately, much of the world's population doesn't look at life with an eternal perspective. Many individuals feel caught in the midst of an unpleasant cycle and never decode the pattern.

In fact, this is a lot like life with children. I see them in the midst of a pattern and wonder how long it will take for them to decode it. Like last night when they were dipping lollipops into glasses of water over and over again. Not once did they realize they were giving precious licks away to thankless glasses of water. They just kept dipping and giggling, oblivious.

I hope I'm not in the midst of a pattern, or phase in life, obliviously giving away my licks. I want to be alert and energetic enough to discover the code and capture the lessons I'm meant to learn—especially the ones right before my face.

"There are so many wonders in this world. However, sometimes when we have them constantly before our eyes, we take them for granted. We look, but we don't really see; we hear, but we don't really listen," said Bishop Gérald Caussé. He goes on to advise us, "Never tire of discovering or rediscovering the truths of the gospel. The writer Marcel Proust said, 'The real voyage of discovery consists not in seeking new landscapes but in having new eyes'" ("Is It Still Wonderful to You?" *Ensign*, May 2015, 98–99).

This spiritual thought process helps me open my eyes to see my mothering reruns as they truly are: opportunities, do-overs, chances to discover and rediscover truth, and occasions to do better and become better—to become more like Him.

I flip open the spiral notebook nestled on my nightstand and scribble, "Life on repeat? Discover and rediscover. Don't dip the lollipop; decode the pattern." It may only make sense to me, but that's all I need.

I'm so thankful for Christ's life and Atonement, which make repentance and escape from this world possible. Without Him, second chances would not be an option. Plus, I have a surefire inkling that I won't master this quest for spiritual symbolism in one day. I'll need many days (even decades) to see the divine details in my life as He sees them. I'll have to mentally play the reruns in slow motion to catch the fine-tuned idiosyncrasies of the Spirit, and I'll need never-ending opportunities to learn the lessons that teach me how to become more like my Savior.

YOUR TURN!

What tasks did you cross off your to-do list today that will reappear tomorrow? Think thoroughly and write them down. Next, identify the tasks you usually complete absentmindedly and circle a few to focus on in the upcoming days. Begin your day with a prayer to have your eyes opened to see life as He would have you see it. Then when you're in the midst of those circled, seemingly mundane moments, purposefully focus inward and upward. What heavenly lessons or messages come to mind? It always helps me to allow my mind to wander with purpose, meaning keeping the thoughts in the parameter of the purpose but not too pinned down. Good luck!

You too can prevent. I'm a mommy by day and a freelance writer for health-care organizations by naptime. It's an amazing gig because it allows me to stay at home with my favorite people while my brain soaks up a healthy amount of info. Because I have the opportunity to speak with physicians one-on-one, I hear the ins and outs of diseases, research advancements, the latest treatments, and the ever-evolving health-care system. After more than a decade of health-care writing, I've noticed an overarching theme: preventative health care saves lives.

According to the World Research Foundation, "Most diseases are highly preventable by subscribing to preventive health-care habits" ("Preventative Health Care Helps Everyone," World Research Foundation, accessed May 18, 2015, http://www.wrf.org/preventive-healthcare/preventive-healthcare.php). Research proves that avoiding destructive substances, scheduling routine physical exams, and having age-appropriate screenings all lead to a higher quality of life. The same goes for a lifetime of healthy habits, like eating properly, exercising regularly, and getting adequate sleep.

So what does this have to do with my daily search for divine details?

Mother spots a cup inched too close to the edge, so she slides it back instinctively. She doesn't even notice her fingers guiding the cup to safety because she's already thinking of the next task. She tells her little ones to wash their hands before dinner, put the stick down when running, and pack an extra pair of warm socks for tomorrow's campout. She reminds them to say prayers, read scriptures, and "be nice" to awkward classmates. Ungratefuls call it nagging, but I much prefer "preventing."

A mother serves as a professional preventionist. She aims to avert sickness, injury, pain, and unnecessary sorrow. She simply can't help but love so much. Sure, she won't prevent all sickness, injury, pain, or sorrow (and honestly, she wouldn't want to because those are required elements of God's plan for us), but she might prevent needless aches and pains here and there.

For example, by washing hands before dinner, the family may avoid weeks of the cold being passed between family members. By sliding the full cup away from the counter's edge, she gives the orange juice less of a chance of splattering the walls and requiring a ten-minute cleanup crew. By reminding her novice Boy Scout to toss extra socks in his backpack, she has perhaps helped him avoid the discomfort that comes from hiking in wet socks. And by pulling the pointy stick from her running toddler's hands, perhaps she can avoid a trip to the emergency room for stitches, saving time, money, and pain—a triple threat.

Thinking on a larger, more eternal scale, a mother knows that a lifetime of prevention now can result in an eternity of incomprehensible happiness. Spiritually healthy habits like scripture study, meditation, church attendance, service, talent development, family home evening, adhering to strong values, and self-discipline bolster the soul. Healthy spiritual habits build character, increase our influence for good, and provide strength and safety throughout life's trials and tribulations.

A key to preventative health care is early detection through health-care screenings. By identifying disease in its earliest form, chances of treatment

are more successful. Likewise, a mother often ana-
lyzes, inspects, and examines the children in her
stewardship in attempts to identify the earliest
form of sinful habits. She wants to squirt sanitizer on sinister starters early, before any sneaky
sin becomes deeply engrained.

The body and spirit go hand-in-hand, just like
preventative health-care habits and preventative
spiritual habits. There will be both blessings and
bruises throughout life, but preventative habits
can ensure fewer injuries and less-severe scars.
Thank goodness for Dr. Moms everywhere—and their
preventative watch care.

CHAPTER 4

White Laundry

8:30 a.m.

As my thoughts wrap up about repetition, so does my laundry. A mental ticker counts each item folded, and imaginary applause breaks out as the millionth article of clothing is neatly placed in its pile. I have just one more undershirt to go. Good thing too; the children are getting creative with their morning chores, and vulnerable Eli just entered the girls' hair salon. The strapping young lad will soon don pigtails and pearls, I'm sure. He's in desperate need of a relief pitcher. So to avert the screaming style (well, more screaming than style), I pitch a few dolls with long, silky hair into the bathroom. The girls squeal in delight and are immediately drawn to the unresisting dolls, allowing Eli a run and a manly breath of relief.

Eli's rescue reminds me of others who have stepped up to the plate for me, and I thank Heavenly Father for the relief pitchers in my life. I've been blessed by women who accept the errand of angels, offering me rest, opportunities to refuel, and a shoulder to cry on. It reminds me of my friend Aubry Bennion, creator of Hello Maypole and a relief pitcher to mothers all around her. Aubry doesn't have children of her own yet, but she surely has a mothering heart. "In the Lord's language, the word *mother* has layers of meaning" (Sheri L. Dew, "Are We Not All Mothers?"

24

Ensign, November 2001, 96), and Aubry finds her meaning by offering bright smiles, playful antics, and helping hands to the exhausted, downtrodden, and overwhelmed mothers around her. She takes seriously the covenant to love one another and bear one another's burdens. For example, when her best friend's son experiences frightening seizures and throws up violently, Aubry runs for paper towels and claims the unglamorous but much appreciated cleanup duty. When shopping with a tired mama friend, Aubry distracts the kids by bouncing balls in the aisles so the mama can focus on shopping for a minute. She *is* that fresh-faced doll who provides relief and reinforcement.

When I asked Aubry about her supportive role, she quickly quoted the proverb, "Thee lift me and I'll lift thee, and we'll ascend together." And then smiling she noted, "We can all lift each other. We have no need to tear each other down—that doesn't help anything! We just need to give relief and be mindful of each other as we navigate our lives, side by side." She's right on target. As mothers, we're all on the same team, and teamwork will surely bring more joy and progress along the journey.

Aubry's example makes me want to be more of a relief to my teammates—to cheer them on and step in when needed. Plus, it brings great comfort to know that our team of mother hearts has the same wise and loving team captain. He is the one and only lifter who can provide eternal relief.

While my thoughts turn toward Him, I count six piles of neatly folded whites lining our bed and spread the remaining white undershirt flat. Gently lifting one sleeve over and then the next, I press creases down and then tuck and fold the shirt into a tight rectangle. When I pick it up, I think of another pile of linens: the white linens Peter found lying in an empty tomb on the first Easter morning.

As it says in Luke 24:12, "Then arose Peter, and ran unto the sepulchre; and stooping down, he beheld the linen clothes laid by themselves, and departed, wondering in himself at that which was come to pass."

To me, the remnant clothes are a kind token, a love note, left behind by the Savior. It seems this was a way to let His wondering disciples know He did not leave in haste. He was there, and He accomplished His assigned task. He was not forced from the tomb during a raid, but He was lovingly doing what He always did—His Father's will. Maybe when I leave neatly folded piles of clothes on beds, waiting for other hands to swoop them up and place them in correct drawers, I am leaving tokens of love too. My love note says, "Mom was here. I did this small task for you, and I'll be there for you again and again."

I imagine Christ's linens folded carefully and set apart from where His body had been. Perhaps He left them behind to show He had moved on from this world but would not leave us alone in the world. Or perhaps the gesture of leaving worldly linens behind indicated to the disciples that He was pleased to leave the world behind. For we know He had been in the world but not of the world, and in one of the most beautiful prayers ever offered He directly states, "And now I am no more in the world, but these are in the world. . . . They are not of the world, even as I am not of the world" (John 17:11, 16).

He lived carefully so as to do His Father's will, and during His mortal ministry He was set apart, like those linens set apart in the tomb—saved for a unique and special purpose.

This notebook is coming in handy. This time I pencil in, "Piles of laundry, like Christ's love-note linens, represent tokens of love and a reminder to set myself apart from the world."

I can't fully comprehend all He went through for me and every member of the human family, and my purpose will not come close to comparing with His, in eternal impact. Yet each soul does have a special purpose with eternal impact, and I'm thankful I can look to His example of how to live.

As I place the last folded white shirt on the top of the heap, I smile. The tedious task of folding laundry and the glory of my Savior intertwined today. That's a first for me. Christ tells us, in Moses 6:63, "All things bear record of me." Truly, all things testify of Christ, if we seek for the divine and spiritual symbols in them—even folding laundry.

YOUR TURN!

Consider Christ. Think of Him while you tackle today's to-dos. He's there, in every blank checkbox, just waiting to be found. Can you find Him? What is He saying to you? Remember, no standard answers exist. Your symbols or lessons will be divinely designed and uniquely suited to your needs at this time. Record the divine details of your day-to-day, and fill your heart with delight as you discover Him.

Wait for me. Once again, I'm waiting impatiently at the front door for stragglers to slip on socks and shoes. Even with a gracious fifteen-minute warning and specific instructions to use the restroom and have jackets and appropriate footwear on, the chances of everyone bounding to the minivan in a synchronized manner are slim to none. Someone can't find her jacket. Another person never left her toys to locate her socks. One stares obliviously at a book, completely unaware that we're going out and about; that's the youngest tot. Could it be because their attention spans are as long as their pinky toes? I'm not sure. I've heard mothers threaten, "Hurry up, or we'll leave without you." That fallacious warning doesn't go over well at our house. It just sends my young ones into a frantic tizzy and tears, and I'd never want my children to think I would really leave them behind. So for now I just cheer them on, with a little nudge here and a helping hand there.

Divine details: It's the same for our new converts. Their testimonies are still young and vulnerable, the worldly ways they've been accustomed to for years beckon to distract, and they desperately need members to patiently cheer them on at the front door. I know this because I'm a convert. My family and I converted from Catholicism when I was fifteen years old. I now laugh at what my family and I didn't fully realize during our first decade or so in the Church. This new life and religion came with so many rules—and new rules within rules. I'm thankful for those accepting members who remained steadfast at the front door, teaching us by word and example.

One time when I was sixteen years old, an adult woman from Church came to visit my mom and inquired where I was. My mom naively stated that I was back in my bedroom with a boy from school. The sister spoke right up, gently but directly teaching my mother ways to help her teenage daughter maintain virtue. A few minutes later my mom knocked on my bedroom door and announced, "There's a new rule in our house . . ." If this concerned sister, and the many other helpful Church members, had bit their tongues instead of extending their arms and advice, we may have fallen by the way and been left behind. I'm thankful they were patient with us, gave us nudges and cheers, and never threatened to move forward without us. I'm thankful for Church members who may have received the gospel first but wait with long-suffering for those of us who received it last.

"The first shall be last, and . . . the last shall be first" (D&C 29:30).

CHAPTER 5

Grocery Store Stories

9:00 a.m.

During fall, winter, and spring, this time of day is prime learning time. But because our humble homeschool is technically out for spring break and our cupboards and refrigerator are looking quite bare, my little people and I load up in the minivan for a grocery-store gamble. I say gamble, because I can't guarantee how public outings will turn out. We've had plenty of perfectly pleasant and uneventful public appearances—but the less-pleasant ones worry me.

For example, once while in the middle of the mall, three bodily functions happened simultaneously, though to separate children. Child one sneezed a long goober of green mucus that hung from her nose to her toes. It was impressively disgusting. Newly potty-trained child two clutched her private parts and performed a moving rendition of the classic potty dance. Crocodile tears pooled in the corners of her eyes, and the nearest public restroom was not near at all. And last, the bubbly boy had his second blowout diaper of the day. A brown streak shot up his onesie to the nape of his neck and also dripped down his chubby thighs. Meanwhile, the nearly empty diaper bag sat stranded in the minivan. Oh, the horror—my horror and the horror of the many onlookers.

I remember when I was pregnant with my first child. Onlookers at the grocery store graciously opened doors when I approached; they'd notice my protruding belly and initiate conversations with questions of when the blessed babe would make its arrival. Some even gave my tummy an unsolicited rub, and others volunteered to escort me back to the car and unload my cart. People were so kind!

When I became obviously pregnant with my second child and had one angelic pony-tailed tot squeaking in the front of the cart, people continued their sweet ways, but at a slightly less animated intensity. Their main concern was if a baby boy would arrive to "balance" our family. When I'd reveal another girl was on the way, a sympathetic pout swooped across strangers' faces. Often they'd ask if I'd try again for that hoped-for boy. Honestly, this oft-repeated conversation bothered me. I worried my little girl in the cart would pick up on their responses and associate a negative connotation with welcoming a sister.

Still, occasionally a generous grocery store attendee would ask, "Would you like any help with your bags today?" or another store patron would give me a supportive smile.

But when I became pregnant with number three, I noticed a striking change in support levels. Instead of wanting to assist the little mama with the large tummy and two girls squished under heaps of groceries in the cart, people found it much more entertaining to watch. I could almost hear them thinking, "Let's see how she's going to do this," while I maneuvered the cart and tots through crowds and sharp turns. People blatantly gawked. Some smiled, some scowled, but everyone seemed to stare. My life became a mesmerizing reality show—and we've been starring in it ever since.

So to please our captive audiences, I make sure that when we leave our home we look presentable. We trade mismatched sweatpants for coordinating outfits. All children and their mama sport intentional hairstyles, weather-appropriate footwear, and our best manners while at the store—or at least we try.

With one child in the basket, one buckled in the child seat, and one hanging onto the side of the cart, we're a large load. With those three small bodies added together, I'm nearly pushing my body weight before we even add groceries. That's what I call a mommy workout.

On this morning we begin our scavenger hunt in the produce section. Like most youngsters, mine are hands-on learners. They want to feel each avocado, smell the pineapples, and pick out the perfect bananas. The four-year-old grips the grocery list as if it were a treasure map.

The toddler enthusiastically identifies what he can, proclaiming with a loud voice, "Oranges! Oranges! Oranges!" The six-year-old runs ahead to gather plastic bags, daydreaming of grocery shopping by herself one day.

Trying to work my spiritual symbolism spell, I imagine the plan of salvation laid out like a grocery list, with heavenly ordinances that are required before "checking out" of this life.

A few minutes later while my eldest weighs a selection of brightly colored peppers, an older lady approaches us.

She warmly smiles and coos, "What gorgeous children you have." Bright beams of pride erupt from the praise. My children immediately sit up straighter and look this stranger in the eye with cordial hellos.

It feels like this is going to be an exceptional grocery shopping experience after all. With a spring in my step, we head toward the bread section. In the middle of the aisle we encounter another woman, and due to my wide load, we need to politely excuse ourselves in order to pass by. This woman doesn't smile, though. In fact, she unashamedly eyes me up and down multiple times and eyes each of my children.

"You have my deepest sympathies," she sneers.

What? Did that just happen? I am sure my facial expression appears puzzled, but thanks to the previous encounter and my children's good behavior, I have enough brawn and brains to quickly rebuttal, "I'm having a blast and wouldn't want it any other way."

She smirks and slithers on. Her scrutinizing eyes and odd remark leave me agitated. I feel my heart rate increase while I contemplate better comebacks; I wonder what spurred on such unnecessary and unpleasant commentary. My kids are all being well-behaved. I decide it couldn't have been that. Was it due to personal circumstances? Does she have a pack of wolf-children at home who torment her? Had she been terrible to her parents as a youth and now deeply fears retaliation?

As luck would have it, we turn up the next aisle to reconvene.

"I didn't mean to insult you," she says.

That was sweet of her. I forgive her and let her know it's all right. Then curiosity gets the best of me, and I ask if she has any children of her own.

"Heck no!" (I'm censoring.) Okay, that was harsh. "I have a cat. That's my baby."

"Huh," is all I can muster.

She keeps talking. "I do like children, but I just wouldn't want to be around them twenty-four hours a day," she says to the stay-at-home mother of three.

I want to cover my children's ears! I wish I boldly testified of the joy they bring—the innocence, excitement for life, genuine emotions, and pure love. Or how the sacrifices made in behalf of motherhood are repaid threefold simply by their heavenly presence. Instead, I manage a complicated 180 with the cart in search of the most direct escape route. She bids farewell and leaves me with calls of another, "I hope I didn't insult you," and a "to each their own" justification.

The conversation loops on replay in my mind while I go through the check-out line. I still feel flabbergasted. I try to shake it off but fail. As I load my edible cargo and my most precious cargo for our return trip, out of the corner of my eye I spot Chatty Catty Lady exiting the store.

Blue medical scrubs drape over her spiny frame, her gray-streaked hair is pulled back tight (like her temperament), and she looks, well, she looks worn. Thick glasses weigh heavy on her face, perhaps representing a life weighed down with troubled times. She slowly approaches an old, beaten down vehicle with the last specks of paint peeled back, revealing only cold, hard, rusty metal; possibly a parallel to the harsh effects of her troubled life.

I imagine the woman returning home to a quiet, dark, and dreary residence, with only a feline family member to greet her. No wonder she comes across more bitter than sweet. I instantly wish her a more cheerful life, one full of color, eruptive giggles, tight hugs, and a forever family.

All I can think is, "*You* have my deepest sympathies." And I mean it.

What a change a glance across the parking lot makes! The lengthened distance grants a fresh viewpoint and an opportunity for the Spirit to whisper symbolism to my snubbed heart. That symbolism changed the color of my day and penned a new story in my heart, line upon line.

Almost miraculously, the newly acquired character background reclassifies the woman I once labeled as villain to victim— or even neglected heroine. My heartstrings pull, and any residue of hardheartedness from our encounter melts into authentic empathy.

My thoughts, sprinkled with symbolism, cruise by at such lightening speeds that I barely notice it happening: love abounds.

"We must remember that those mortals we meet in parking lots, offices, elevators, and elsewhere are that portion of mankind God has given us to love and to serve. It will do us little good to speak of the general brotherhood of mankind if we cannot regard those who are all around us as our brothers and sisters," said Spencer W. Kimball ("Jesus: The Perfect Leader," *Ensign*, August 1979).

As I think about it, telling myself a story is an entertaining game I play often to alter my emotions and perspective—whether I am aware of it or not. When a vehicle zooms past mine with reckless speed and maneuvers, I'll think to myself, "I sure hope that driver gets to the hospital in time to kiss his wife before she goes into surgery." Stories like that make road rage vanish, and I find myself rooting for the driver.

Of course, it's much easier to tell myself a story when the main characters are strangers.

One of my precious daughters tests my patience every time her trademark moan erupts. It drags from the back of her throat, stringing out longer and louder the more disgruntled she feels. Though it sounds like she's in pain, it's really inflicting pain on the listener.

If I say, "Darling, you need to finish your morning chores

before breakfast," her response usually entails her head thrown back and a loud "Uhhhhhhhhhh!" that looks and sounds a lot like a sick seal. How do I tell myself a story there? And that's just a little thing; I can only imagine the drama, and even the tragedies, the future may hold.

The more trying the individual and circumstances, the greater the distance required to see—or so I imagine. I love the biblical account of Zacchaeus, a short, wealthy man with faith in Jesus Christ. When Jesus passed through Jericho, crowds of people filled the streets, and Zacchaeus, being short in stature, couldn't see his Savior. Yet Zacchaeus proved to be resourceful and determined; he put forth great effort to elevate himself by climbing a nearby sycamore tree to see Christ (Luke 19:4). For trials of faith involving others, I often find myself a short in spiritual stature and need to put forth grander efforts to earn an elevated, more eternal viewpoint. On occasion, I may need to climb *way* up or step *way* back—to the pre-earth life if necessary—to see the ultimate beginning of the story.

Zeniff from the Book of Mormon is another example of changing perceptions—and even saving lives—by seeing the good in others. He was preparing his army of Nephites to attack the Lamanites and destroy them, but before he did, he sent spies among them. I wonder what those spies reported. Whatever the report was, it told Zeniff a new story. He says, "But when I saw that which was good among them I was desirous that they should not be destroyed" (Mosiah 9:1). Isn't that all it takes—seeing some good in others—to change hearts?

Finding elements of good in others can soften our own hearts and, in a way, save our own lives. By introducing our stories with a correct identification of the main character as a child of God, valiant enough in the first estate to receive a body and mortal experience, we can attempt to see past hardened hearts, hurtful words, and hopelessness. We can recognize the good within them. We may not fully comprehend what has caused their current hardened hearts, but we can know they once began soft and good, and we can remember their divine worth. "Remember the worth of souls is great in the sight of God" (D&C 18:10).

I adore how masterful storytellers add details to capture the hearts of their listeners. The details add splashes of creatively placed color to black-and-white images—and suddenly those stories' images, ideas, and situations come to life. I have a friend from San Diego named Aarean Jergensen who feels mesmerized and motivated by color. She's fascinated with color's effect on the psyche, and she's magnetically drawn to hues in nature and every-day life. In fact, she loves color so much that a few years ago she began the Color Issue blog and online presence. With her camera and eye for detail, she points out the splashy spectrum of color that makes life beautiful.

The other day, Aarean told me that her search for color increases her love of the little things in life, fosters her creativity, and makes her a better mother. I feel that telling myself a story to see spiritual moments in everyday doings adds crucial color too. It increases love, nurtures spiritual sight, and beautifies souls. In the end, seeing colorful, spiritual details helps me become a better mother, teacher, and believer.

Aarean's color love began as a child, when her father would point out the beauty in things around them. He'd say, "Look at that purple sunset!" and "Did you notice the turquoise gleaming from the bird's feathers?" Her dad diligently desired to inspire his children to notice details normally overlooked and appreciate the colorful beauty often taken for granted. Those details added insight to his children's stories and perspective. Now Aarean con-sciously passes down that attention to and appreciation for detail to her children.

Likewise, I want to pass down the skills I'm learning to my children! I want their lives to feel colorful and full of spiritual life. I want them to be moved by the stories surrounding them and to gift them with storytelling talents. With that said, it's vital that I follow Aarean's father's lead by pointing out the colorful beauty I see—to share the stories, the spiritual sightings, and the divine details swirling around our spirits. I know that as I make this a purposeful priority in my life, His lessons, symbols, and messages will be revealed to me and my children. He will help us see the true story—His story—and His story will mold our hearts.

YOUR TURN!

Time to tell a story. For your first one, pick a small trial or event that bothers you. Say a prayer, requesting His sight, and then open your mind and heart. It's tricky to leave personal opinions and feelings on the curb, but it will allow your outlook to expand and fresh colors to be added. This tactic may require deep levels of empathy to broaden your perspective and will likely require more than one attempt. Find a peaceful place to ponder. Search the scriptures. Pray again. Soon you'll see the good, and you'll experience the sweetness that comes from storytelling.

Not-so-pretend play. One of the reasons I love homeschooling is because it seems to extend my children's childhood while preparing them for the next stage in life. For example, nearly every day they spend significant time deeply engaged in imaginary worlds. They often choose settings like school (even directly after school!), house, never-never land, or a restaurant. Lately their favorite place is a pretend town called "Flower Bed"—complete with democratic president, friendly storekeeper, and, of course, many families. Families appear as central to their pretend world as they are to this world. In fact, I've noticed the core to my children's pretend play is founded on real life. They prepare for their approaching future by thinking, understanding, and acting it out.

Divine details: Likewise, we go to the temple to prepare for our future. Though there are different settings and ordinances available to participate in, all prepare us to stand in the presence of God—a future as real and faraway-feeling to us as adulthood is to a child. In the temple we spend significant time thinking, understanding, and even acting on behalf of others to prepare ourselves, and those who have passed on to the next life before us, to stand in the presence of our God. Really, both our children's imaginative play and our real temple attendance qualify as beneficial and enjoyable preparation for the future. I guess that's one more reason I cherish playdates at His house.

CHAPTER 6

Tuning Out to Tune In

10:00 a.m.

Within just an hour, I feel discombobulated. My initial streak of spiritual thoughts had me excited about my new project, but then life happened and I digressed into my familiar "survival mode."

Crumbs cloud the once-swept floor, tiny hands pound piano keys in a nonsensical tune, our tablet echoes math facts, and my toddler's favorite educational toy caterpillar got stuck sounding out the letter z. The extra busy beehive vibe adds to my frustrations as I search for a lost object—a personal pet peeve.

I planned to update my blog, but for the life of me I can't find the cord to connect the camera with the computer. As I pull apart the downstairs in pursuit, I overhear a frustrated Anna talking to Eli about their next activity. Every time Anna suggests something, like "Let's go to Storyville" or "Let's play Candyland," Eli completes the sentence by shouting, "Dot com!" Anna isn't amused by his fourteen-month-old, Internet-savvy antics. To add an extra splash of crazy, my cell phone sporadically whistles alerts of text messages from fast-fingered young women. They want to know what tomorrow's "mystery dessert" for our midweek Church activity will be. How have they not guessed that when I say "mystery" it means it's a mystery to me? With all the pulling apart, "dot

39

com"ing, and chiming, I feel a strong desire to pull the plugs and shut down my home for an early, all-day nap.

Don't get me wrong, I'm thankful to live in a time and place with technology. I realize millions of people have never sent distant friends personalized happy birthday songs, video chatted with great-grandparents, or found their way to an inconveniently located dentist office by using their GPS device (all of which I have enjoyed within the week). At the same time, keeping up with life in the Information Age also comes with disadvantages. The biggest drawback I've found: I can't hear myself think. Seriously. The constant onslaught of images and the world's opinion blaring through every speaker seems impossible to block. Satan is well aware, and he's taking every opportunity to use today's luxurious technology to distract Heavenly Father's children from their divine missions.

I remember a quote by Elder Richard G. Scott that says, "Have you noticed how Satan works to capture the mind and emotions with flashing images, blaring music, and the stimulation of every physical sense to excess? He diligently strives to fill life with action, entertainment, and stimulation so that one cannot ponder the consequences of his tempting invitations" (Richard G. Scott, "How to Live Well amid Increasing Evil," *Ensign*, May 2004).

It's so true! I find myself trapped in a surround-sound lifestyle. Worldly static slips into nearly every aspect of my daily routine. Children zone-out in front of screens in minivans, teens and adults rarely get beyond arm's length of their smarty-pants phones, and every app and social network prods for attention. With the world's soundtrack constantly playing in the background of life, it's no surprise that Satan cunningly desires the starring role of guest DJ. He aims to be our pied piper, luring souls to dance away from the straight and narrow path, while clapping in time to his dark, demented beat.

"The adversary tries to smother [us] with a multitude of loud, persistent, persuasive, and appealing voices." That's why we must "filter out the static generated by Satan," as President James E. Faust admonished us ("Voice of the Spirit," *Ensign*, June 2006, 4, 6).

I remember when my husband talked me into the latest and

greatest cell phone on the market—our first smart phone. At first, we gushed over the bells and whistles. Within seconds, we could access bank accounts, read the latest news headlines, or preview the menu of a local restaurant. I felt connected and in the loop. But questions kept nudging me: What exactly am I connected to? Whose loop have I entered in? Is it wise to carry the noise and distractions of cyberspace in my back pocket?

Elder Richard G. Scott warns us, "Be wise in how you embrace technology. . . . Doing all we can to invite the gentle, guiding influence of the Holy Ghost into our lives is critical in our attempts to center our homes on the Savior" ("For Peace at Home," *Ensign*, May 2013, 30).

The scriptures teach that the Holy Ghost communicates in a still, small voice—the exact opposite of Satan's tactics. As a busy mom, I have a hard enough time hearing my own rambling thoughts throughout the day (as you can probably tell by my rambling thoughts on these pages). Understanding and being enlightened by a hushed voice offers double the challenge.

Of course, I'd much rather hear and be led by the Holy Ghost's message for me than listen to my own thoughts—or worse, Satan's nasty noises. And if I want to conquer my quest to discover the divine details in my daily life, I desperately need to hear the Spirit whispering to me. So I decide it's time give the still, small voice a chance to be heard.

When I envision "still," I see still waters. More specifically, I imagine a turquoise-blue pond in the middle of Mother Nature's most secluded forest. A lily pad or two rests on top of the water, but that's about it. I can stand near the edge of the crystal-clear water and see even the deepest sections of white-pebbled floor. Not a fish swims. Nothing moves. It is still.

My life today is nothing like that pond. It's not still *at all*. If I truly want to hear more whisperings of the still, small voice, I need to dedicate time for sweet, sacred stillness.

Once, I served as a music leader for children and tried to teach this principle to our congregation's wiggly cherubs. I stood at the front of the room and instructed all of our little singers to squirm, sway, and twist in their seats but to lock their mouths shut. While arms waved and legs kicked, I whispered a secret message. After signaling for stillness, I asked what the message was. Not a child in the room had a clue. So we tried again, but this time quiet *and* still, and every child received the message loud and clear.

As President Packer teaches us, "The Spirit does not get our attention by shouting or shaking us with a heavy hand. Rather it whispers. It caresses so gently that if we are preoccupied we may not feel it at all. (No wonder that the Word of Wisdom was revealed to us, for how could the drunkard or the addict feel such a voice?)" (Boyd K. Packer, "The Candle of the Lord," *Ensign*, January 1983, 53).

Yes, the addictions are real and overpowering—whether we're addicted to drugs, drinks, sugar, technology, or whatever. Fighting for freedom from those addictions provides freedom to hear Him, to feel Him, and to choose Him.

Looks like I need to apply that lesson to my own life, and I think that lesson will prove to be a useful tool in my pursuit of everyday symbolic **mom**ents. So I surrender my failing search for the USB cord and seek my spiritual spiral notebook instead. I commit to eliminate excessive clamor and background static and to reevaluate consuming addictions. I set a goal to look for times each day to sit still and ponder sacred subjects.

Adding another bullet point, I write, "Tune out to tune in."

Some of my first ideas for tuning out unnecessary clamor include limiting time spent perusing social network sites, driving without music on, silencing digital background noise while completing household chores, and only touching my phone when necessary. And then there is one bad habit that should never have started: shoveling food toward my little tykes while we stare like zombies into the ever-present black box. No more. I resolve to tune out the world in order to tune in to the Spirit.

YOUR TURN!

Here are three simple ways to tune out to tune in:

1. Select one tech habit to sacrifice and replace with stillness.
2. Dedicate a specific space for your favorite devices so that you're not physically and mentally attached to them.
3. Get the whole family on board. Work together to select one hour each day when the family can tune out technology and tune in to one another.

Tea towels and my Savior. While I fill a glass of water at the refrigerator water dispenser, I ask the kiddos to gather library books that need to be returned. That quickly, the clear water spills over the glass and gushes to the floor. Grabbing an old flour sack tea towel, I kneel down for a quick clean up—and that's when I realize that Christ is like my absorbent tea towel. When my emotions overflow and I kneel down in prayer to Him, He has the ability to absorb those feelings and clean up the mess. It happened to me recently when I got upset and said something I shouldn't have to someone I love dearly. I knelt in prayer and cried to Him about it, and He absorbed my messy feelings—the ones that had allowed such biting words to leave my mouth. All that was left was a shiny, clean heart. I'm thankful for tea towels and my Savior.

CHAPTER 7

Cottage Cheese, Please

Noon

Strapped into his high chair with a plastic bib around his neck, my fourteen-month-old scowls one second and stretches a smile across his face the next. He's in one of those moods. He woke up in a twisted position from his morning nap, and now I have the "opportunity" to entertain this twisted disposition. It's snack time, and since the reheated chicken tenders weren't a big hit, I present a kitchen staple: cottage cheese.

"Would you like some cottage cheese?" I coo.

He nods a big yes with his toothy grin.

Though our conversations are generally one-sided from a verbal standpoint, we have quite the communication system going. He's learned several keywords in American Sign Language (with meal-time vocabulary including "all done," "food," "more," "please," and "water"), but as his mother, I'm his number-one interpreter. I've watched his uninhibited thought process since day one. I wouldn't say I can read his mind or that I know what he'll do in every situation, but by spending every developmental day with him, I receive matchless insight. I can translate the tiniest grunt, know what he's signing without looking at him, or predict which forbidden cupboard he's headed for next. I think on the minutest level it must be similar to Heavenly Father's omniscient ability to allow His

45

children agency while simultaneously foreseeing our decisions to each trying situation.

I pull up the worn blue stool next to his seat and deliver the first scoop of cottage cheese. *SWACK!* Just like that, his left arm swings out and tips the spoon and his favorite food onto the floor. Okay, I didn't see that coming; so much for the all-knowing mom talk. But, wow, what a simple and powerful display of independence. With the smack of the spoon, I realize he wants to feed himself. Not the most pleasant form of body language, but he gets his point across. Feeding himself has become one of his utmost challenging and fulfilling activities. I'm a bit of a clean freak (that's an understatement), so I usually only permit self-feeding with substances that stick well to the spoon, like mashed potatoes. With that in mind, I begin mentally debating the next course of action.

Normally, if he lets me feed him, the side dish can be devoured in three minutes. But we don't have anywhere to go, and he does need to learn this skill. But at the same time, he shouldn't be rewarded for slapping the spoon out of my hands, and he's going to get drenched in the goop, which means a big clean up. . . . The thoughts battle it out in my head until I surrender the spoon.

With gleeful delight, he clamps a tight fist around the handle—a classic novice move. I brace myself; it's going to get messy. As his teacher, I know he has the physical capabilities to complete the job. All four digits and opposable thumb are intact and working properly; his bones, muscles, and tendons have formed and developed; and his dexterity is advancing at a rapid rate. He's ready. Even with all the physical preparation, he needs hours and hours of experience before he can proudly be pronounced a self-feeder.

Heavenly Father must feel the same way about us. He's created my spirit, given me a physical body, and miraculously brought me into an earthly home. Even with all that prep, He knows I must live life on earth for a significant period of time before I can ever develop and progress—a requisite to entering into His kingdom. He too knows I'm going to get messy. I need Him to coach me, and I definitely need Him to clean me up. With that perspective, I ease up and decide to enjoy the feeding frenzy.

My chubby tot's first attempt is pure entertainment. A barely visible speck of cottage cheese makes its way from bowl to mouth. His eyes light up and he beams with success. After several similar bites (if I can call them that), he realizes his tummy remains just as hungry as when he began. This isn't working—it's not enough. He gives it a few more goes as I flip through the snail mail on the counter.

"Mom. Mom. Mom," he calls. Yes! It's time for Super Mommy to save the day. I love this part of the job. Pleased he'll let me take control again and get this meal moving, Helicopter Mom comes in for a landing.

"Here, honey, let me help you," I offer. My hand reaches out, and he screeches in disapproval. My help is obviously unwanted. Trying to play it cool and give some space, I back away.

"Mom! Mom! Mom!" The calling proceeds with increased intensity.

Ding! The lightbulb flashes. He doesn't want me to take over; he simply wants to know I am here. He needs a little cheerleading because the task at hand is getting difficult. Oh, how I can relate. Many times I call with intensity to my Heavenly Father in prayer needing just that—reassurance that I can get through whatever bumpy bowl of cottage cheese lies in front of me.

So I cheer him on. I try persuading him to dig a little deeper with the spoon. I even put more cottage cheese in the bowl, thinking that may make it easier to collect. My attention and enthusiastic tone makes a difference. His confidence grows, the undertaking seems easier, and within minutes the bowl is devoured.

"Cheerleading through cottage cheese. We've got to eat it ourselves, but He's cheering us on with every bite," I jot down in my spiral notebook. I even read it out loud to my small-fry audience member.

Unprompted, my buddy's big blue eyes look up at me. He stares straight into my eyes, gives a little grin, and sweetly signs, "Thank you." I am not joking. It seems so unreal! The unanticipated gratitude feels heaven-sent, and the silent "thank you" speaks loudly to my soul. I wish I had captured the moment on video! Let's face it, like all mothers, most of my day is spent in the service of children, and an unprompted, genuine thank-you is extremely rare. I truly didn't expect it. The gesture feels as if Heavenly Father thanked me for pausing my thoughts in attempts to replace them with His. It feels as if He thanked me for my efforts in our partnership of raising His children. My whole heart swells.

The thanks absolutely makes my day, and with that, I wonder how often I thank my Heavenly Father for His efforts and love. I think about how He must feel when I stop and sincerely offer thanks and praise—especially for the divine details. I vow to express my sincere appreciation more regularly and instantaneously.

After my eyes open from a thank-you prayer, I sit back amazed. "Just another meal" is transformed into a cherished moment. As my mind tunes out the surrounding earthly static, my eyes open and I'm blessed with morsels of spiritual nourishment in between the real bites my son is taking. Just like with snacking, each bite-sized morsel adds up. Today, I have received many nibbles of spiritual nourishment by permitting the Holy Ghost to enter my mind and lead my thoughts.

I place the container of cottage cheese back in the fridge because both Eli and I feel full.

My spiral notebook quickly fills up with bullet points like these:

- Guessing Eli's next moves gives a tiny glimpse into Heavenly Father's all-knowing power.
- Cheerleading through cottage cheese. We've got to eat it ourselves, but He's cheering us on with every bite.
- A little thank-you goes a long way; increase acts of gratitude to Heavenly Father.
- As calories add up with every bite, testimonies add up with bite-sized spiritual lessons.

YOUR TURN!

He's cheering you on too! Have you noticed? Make a list of specific, personal blessings from Heavenly Father. Add to it daily. As you recognize His gifts, you will feel His love and deep desire for your success. How do you thank Him for such an outpouring? Perhaps it's time to try a new form of gratitude. Here are some ideas: write a thank-you prayer to Him in your journal, initiate a thank-a-thon during the next family home evening, or pick a blessing you could pass on to someone else.

"Did we say a prayer?" mumbles a child with her mouth full, only a minute after *she* said, "Amen." We all look at her blank face and realize she is sincerely asking. I want to knock her noggin and wake her up a bit. The sad thing is, I'm guilty of it too. I had to second-guess myself earlier this morning when wondering if I had I taken my daily vitamins or not. I couldn't recall what time Avery's piano lessons were (and I took her thirty minutes early the week before). Just recently I fried a bowl of oatmeal in the microwave because I completely forgot to add milk! It's as if I'm walking through life with an extra and translucent eyelid, making it possible to appear present but I'm really sleeping behind the lens.

Personalized spiritual symbolism: Take the scales off of those eyes and pay close attention to my spiritual day and temporal day. If I'll live through the day either way, I might as well open my eyes to the lessons surrounding me! Just think of Saul. Being spiritually blind to the true meaning of his mortal mission, he devoted himself to persecuting the Church. After Christ appeared to Saul and asked him why, Saul was physically blinded for three days until a disciple named Ananias healed him: "And immediately there fell from his eyes as it had been scales: and he received sight forthwith" (Acts 9:18).

Removing my scales is like removing my contact lenses: I must open my eyes wide and, with tiny movements, make the change. My tiny movements started this morning by looking at the tiny moments in my mommy day in a new way. I'm seeing a change already. I will adhere my faith to the promise Elder

Neil L. Andersen recently gave: "As you keep the commandments and pray in faith to see the Lord's hand in your life, I promise you that He will open your spiritual eyes even wider, and you will see more clearly that you are not alone" ("Thy Kingdom Come," *Ensign*, May 2015, 121–22).

Lose the plate, lose the food. I crave warm-weather lunches all year long. I love the way the rainbow of fresh food splashes across plates in spring and summertime. By displaying foods according to color, they appear vibrant and lively. When admiring the peach pieces, purple grapes, freshly picked strawberries, avocado chunks, sliced cheese, and grainy crackers, I see my testimony of the gospel. Each food type is a separate gospel principle. The peaches may represent the Restoration; the grapes symbolize revelation from modern prophets; strawberries could be priesthood power. Most important, Jesus Christ is the all-encompassing plate. If the plate drops, so does all the food—and I completely ruin my meal. On the other hand, when beginning my meal with an empty plate, my stomach hungers to fill that plate with an array of delicious food waiting on the kitchen counter. Yum! Let's feast!

CHAPTER 8

Weeds or Wildflowers

H ere in Oregon, we treasure sunshine. When the rain lets up and sunrays dry the almost-always-damp grass, families march outdoors quicker than ants to a picnic. Seeing the glorious afternoon awaiting us, we eagerly dress in grubby clothes and head outside for some vitamin D. Queen Katie, our Jack Russell Terrier, and the children immediately begin exploring every inch of the backyard, easily entertained by the refreshing atmosphere. Tree-huggers at heart, they throw themselves into nature—literally. It must have been part of an undercover, commando hide-and-seek game.

I decide to take advantage of their independence and return to an unfinished project. Kneeling in direct sunlight, I continue removing winter's leftovers and spring's unwanted vegetation. A small section of cleared soil from last week's attempt stands out in comparison to the dried leaves, green weeds, and faded debris that cover the rest of the yard. Unfortunately, in the week or two since I last squatted here, several annoying sprouts have already invaded the once cleared area. I look closer, disgusted to see that the scrawny greens managed to sprout so tall in a mere week's time. Those little buggers grow fast! What good is weeding if the unwelcome seedlings return before I graduate to the next section?

So before starting a new area, I set to spiffing up the initial clearing. I wonder about the spiritual significance in this banal task. Hm. It's a good thing I don't purify my spiritual garden in the same manner. If I worked to perfect a specific weakness before progressing to the next gospel principle, my testimony, talents, and progress would be unproductive and severely limited.

The thoughts remind me of an admirable Church member my husband met during his mission. This man kept the commandments in the same manner he compiled his financial budget. The gentleman developed and maintained a spreadsheet of character traits and gospel principles, and each night he'd analyze his day, tracing the rows and columns with his fingertips and rating himself on his daily achievements and setbacks. I imagine what that would be like for a minute, taking my finger and pretending to locate the spreadsheet's first column, honesty, and then thinking about every interaction of the day before rating myself. The next column is virtue, then service, and then faith. For this gentleman, the meticulous methodical system improved his daily repentance process, strengthened his weaknesses, and focused his life on the path toward perfection.

I bring my attention back to the many budding weeds; they look so innocent. Although I'm tempted to save time and energy by looking past the scrawny sprouts and focusing today's efforts on clearing out larger debris, I know if I do, a week later those gangly things will double their strength and multiply like, well, like weeds. Calling upon my challenge to see divinity in the details, I decide the lesson I need in my life revolves around the ease of turning my head to look past scrawny sins. Like the man from Alex's mission, I need to be better about identifying those sins and getting to work.

It's an unpopular message in today's instant-gratification-obsessed world. Society suggests solving personal problems with retail therapy, "me time," or other bandage approaches that mask symptoms but ignore the heart of the matter. And sadly, I've bought into it. After a rough week of not being the mom I could have and should have been, I yearn for a favorite department store diversion. I dream of an escape within a particular fashion retail palace that smells like style and feels like paradise—but stands as a foundationless great and spacious building. I know it won't bring lasting happiness. I know the pair of ludicrously expensive designer jeans would diminish my bank account and increase the severity of consequences awaiting me. But after I've already ruined the week at home, it's tempting to ruin the week financially too. Likewise, sin grows upon sin, and if never uprooted, it leaves a web of tangled roots around our souls.

Amulek testifies of this principle in Alma 34:33–34:

> I beseech of you that ye do not procrastinate the day of your repentance until the end; for after this day of life, which is given us to prepare for eternity, behold, if we do not improve our time while in this life, then cometh the night of darkness wherein there can be no labor performed.
>
> Ye cannot say, when ye are brought to that awful crisis, that I will repent, that I will return to my God. Nay, ye cannot say this; for that same spirit which doth possess your bodies at the time that ye go out of this life, that same spirit will have power to possess your body in that eternal world.

I pull the spiral notebook from my back pocket and scribble, "Don't look away. Weed those sprouting sins now."

As I kneel in work, pondering the symbolism just discovered in the menial process of weeding, I remember a small decorative sign along the sidewalk leading to the back door of my parents' home. Swaying above soil and hanging on an iron rod, a shiny blue plaque reads, "May all your weeds be wildflowers." Below the sign, scattered weeds and wildflowers sprout energetically toward the sun and topple out of a decomposing brown barrel. My mother is quite clever (and she's one of my all-time favorite people too).

If I looked at the bucket of weeds without seeing or reading the sign I'd probably think my parents had a bit of yard work to do. When the sprouts grew to full bushels, I'd probably wonder why my folks were letting their beautiful yard "go to pot," as my mother would say. But by reading the optimistic sign, so strategically placed, I instead admire those baby weeds. In fact, I found myself smiling at their budding greens.

Taking the weed symbolism on an entirely different route, I

wonder if that catchy phrase could relate to the obnoxious weeds in my mothering and housekeeping repertoire—not the spiritual sins, of course, but the unwanted or wild tasks growing in my unique soil. Personally, I'd like to uproot cleaning the toilet, cooking, and cleaning up after a million meals each day (I'm only slightly exaggerating). So how in the world could I view those personal weeds as wildflowers? Then it clicks. I just need to keep up exactly what I set out this day to do! By discovering the divine details in each weed, I can in fact turn it into an optimistic, helpful, colorful, fragrant wildflower!

The more I think about it, the more sure I am that this new theory can really work! For instance, rather than dry heaving when sanitizing a soiled toilet, I'd focus my thoughts on revealing the divine details within the task. As it promises in the Book of Mormon, "All things denote there is a God" (Alma 30:44). I start chuckling as I picture a cartoon toilet scrub brush removing muck and revealing a shiny spiritual thought. Ha! It's already working.

Being so captivated by my own imagery and compulsively consumed with picking the weeds, I realize that I haven't looked up in the past few minutes to see what the children are doing. And then it hits me: that brick-in-the-gut panic feeling that every mother fears.

Where's Eli?

I sprint to the side of the house. The gate is still closed, but from between the fence planks, I see my toddler busting out of the fenced yard and down the driveway toward the street. Running to the gate, I scream with fervor, "ELI!" The air fills with the piercing scream of a mother's terror. And though the shrieking alarm feels necessary in the moment, I'd be mortified to watch it on replay.

Hearing his mother scream his name, Eli pauses, glances over his left shoulder nonchalantly, and then picks up the pace. It's like he knows he's gone too far and he's surely in trouble, so he might as well make a break for it and go as far as possible.

Luckily, not a single car speeds by. In fact, other than the echo of my blood-curdling scream, the neighborhood sounds like a ghost town. I run, eventually clasping onto my escapee's shoulders, kneel down, and ask, "Why would you do that? Why? You must stay by Mommy! You scared Mommy." The fear in my voice and eyes impresses the seriousness of the situation.

I carry him back to the middle of the safely guarded backyard, and I sternly tell the older children to keep an eye on the little sprinter. And then guess what Eli does. He immediately turns and bolts toward the gate again! Hello? Did he not just learn that lesson? Why flee again? There's nothing even that fabulous on the other side of the gate!

At this point I have two choices: become unglued because clearly my mothering skills stink as bad as the garbage dumpster near the forbidden fence, or try to find some divinity in the details of this situation to enlighten my caving-in mind. Going with the latter, I mentally struggle for a bit.

And then I wonder how often Heavenly Father mentally struggles when He witnesses my decisions. I'll admit, I've made a handful—or buckets and buckets—of poor decisions, and yes, I've even sinned the same sin more than once or even a thousand times.

Come to think about it, I make awful decisions, earnestly repent (or so I think), and gratefully allow Heavenly Father to swoop me up and place me back into my safe and friendly back-yard—only to bolt from the path, slip past the gate, and run into the dangerous street again.

Yet Heavenly Father doesn't become unglued with me. He continuously gives chances to do better. Lovingly, He swoops in after every fall, kisses my boo-boos, and returns me to safety. He does enforce consequences. He allows falls and injuries, and then He provides another chance.

With that thought, what else could I do but calmly swoop Eli up and start over? This time I add a consequence after the lecture—a time-out strategically placed behind the sliding glass door. He cries and pouts while watching his sisters and dog bound across the lawn. After a few minutes, I return him to the middle of the backyard. This time he makes the right choice—he stays with his family.

It's not always that simple, and I have a feeling that learning opportunities involving my young ones will play out differently than learning opportunities with my teenagers. But I'm thankful for the lessons I need now.

"I will give unto the children of men line upon line, precept upon precept; . . . and blessed are those who hearken unto my precepts, . . . for they shall learn wisdom; for unto him that receiveth I will give more" (2 Nephi 28:30).

We all learn by baby steps.

YOUR TURN!

Are little weeds sprouting in your garden—ones that need plucked before they become overgrown? Are there any wildflowers in your daily repertoire that spiritual symbolism could beautify? Identify one of each (weed and wildflower), and then get moving on your yard work. Remember, it's okay if it's not an instant success. Heavenly Father provides us with many seasons and chances. The key to growth is daily water and sunshine. So seek the Living Water—who also is the Sun, the Son of God.

Cumulus clouds change my form. Lying on Mother Nature's mattress, my trio squints at cumulus clouds floating above. "I see a rabbit!" "I see a pear!" "I see an airplane!" "I see a bear!" I can't resist and quickly find myself alongside their discoveries. A soothing breeze sweeps my bangs to the side, and I take the gust as a signal that there's a divinity to be found in the details of this whimsical game. The rabbit, pear, airplane, and bear change forms in their drift westward on the waves of wind. The children now call those same clouds llama, cupcake, and garter snake, not realizing their previous form.

Heavenly Father, can you see me changing form like these fluffy white clouds? I notice my children morphing, slowly, day by day, forming habits and climbing obstacles. Yours must be a similar way. Looking back at my embarrassingly imprudent sins of decades past, I acknowledge improvement, but am I progressing fast enough? I have so far to go. Yet I apprehensively flex when I consider gusts of wind blowing my direction, to transform my form. I tell myself to relax. Inhale, exhale, and absorb the heaven-sent breezes, gusts, and winds of change.

Work what God gave you. With two hands, Anna smashes her naturally curly hair, pulling it tight against her forehead. "I want straight hair," she whines. But as soon as she lifts her hands, the voluminous locks spring back to full pouf. I try to explain that her hair is absolutely gorgeous and many a girl longs for such tresses. She doesn't buy it. I point out that Heavenly Father gifted her with this special hair, unlike any of the other females in her family (both Avery and I have stick-straight strands). She's not impressed. All she sees is that her hair makes her different. She begs me to braid it, because that proves to flatten it temporarily. I consent.

As my fingers weave her curly strands, a scripture sings to my soul: "For thou art an holy people unto the Lord thy God, and the Lord hath chosen thee to be a *peculiar* people unto himself" (Deuteronomy 14:2; emphasis added).

Lesson learned: I'm supposed to be peculiar—I'm supposed to stand out. I must embrace the characteristics and traits that make me different from others, as long as they make me holy unto the Lord. That could mean my modest apparel, my shunning of foods and drinks against the Word of Wisdom, or my choice to position myself as stay-at-home mom devoted to a traditional marriage. Really, it could mean so many things. Instead of trying to flatten the decisions and traits, cover them up, or "style" them in a more attractive way, I need to work what God gave me. Here's to being peculiar—in perspective and positioning.

Crowning attributes.

When Anna was not even one year old she had a huge mop of dark hair right on top of her forehead—but nowhere else. Wild two-inch curls kinked in every direction. Her tuft reminded me of Elvis's hair.

"What am I supposed to do with this?" I asked an angelic woman in my ward whose gold goddess-like curls drape over her shoulders. She laughed with me but didn't have much advice except to wait it out. As it turns out, her advice proved extremely wise.

Anna's muff turned out to be only the tip of the iceberg. As her hair grew out, we saw what hid under the icy water (or in her case, the scalp). Now

Anna's crazy, curly hair is one of her most crowning physical attributes.

Divine details: Sometimes God gives me crazy kinks in life and I wonder, "What am I supposed to do with this?" I must remind myself that I can't see the whole iceberg—but He can. And oftentimes, by waiting it out and enduring well, those kinks have the potential to turn into my most crowning spiritual attributes.

CHAPTER 9

Listen to Learn

2:00 p.m.

After a power nap, my brood and I conjure up a new adventure. We plan to venture on a field trip, but first we need to freshen up a bit. Avery sits nearby, finishing her favorite story book, while Eli sprints up and down the hallway clutching a football; I practice my French braiding skills on Anna. The braid ends up looking sloppy, but it'll do.

Uh-oh. Where did the rubber band to secure the braid go? Carefully, I hold the braid tight while Anna and I maneuver to the girls' tropical fish–themed bathroom just like we are in a three-legged race (the braid acting as our third leg). Meanwhile, I overhear Eli begin a new project: emptying the drawer of hair products in the master bathroom. It's a favorite pastime of his. He often takes everything out of drawers (or garbage cans, toy boxes, or cupboards) and then dutifully puts everything back in.

Anna and I stay in the kids' bathroom no longer than one minute. I wrap a bright blue rubber band around her braid, clip a barrette to hold her wispy bangs out of her face, and return to the master bedroom, where we find Eli, in the middle of our carpet, flinging the contents of an unzipped plastic baggie. Small circular red prescription pills fly in every direction.

My heart rate accelerates.

I immediately recognize the anti-inflammatory tablets I borrowed from my in-laws earlier in the summer after having a nasty root-canal experience. They were in a plastic baggie and not a child-proof container. Shame on me!

Running to Eli, I drop down on my knees and examine the situation—all while frantic thoughts speed across my mind like closed-captioned text with emotionally capitalized letters.

"PLEASE say he didn't eat any. He eats everything. He has licked dirt off the sidewalk, so OF COURSE he ate some. How could I leave that bag within arm's reach? DID HE swallow those pills? I don't want to call poison control; I've never had to call before and never wanted to call. . . ."

Eli's fingertips appear smeared with red coating from the drug. But I see no red dye around his mouth. That has to be a good sign.

Desperate words spring from my mouth as I continue the assessment: "Dear Heavenly Father, please let me know if he ate some. In the name of Jesus Christ, amen."

Avery immediately speaks up, "Mom, you can't pray with your eyes open!"

"Yes, sometimes you can," I lamely explain. She nods in acceptance.

I try to coax Eli to open his mouth. "Say, 'Ahhhh!'" No luck. Eli just smiles, only revealing hippo teeth. I stare at him, feeling exasperated and not knowing what to do next.

Avery interrupts, "Mom, what is your Holy Spirit saying to you?"

Oh, my profound peanut-sized professor. The Psalmist spoke truth when he said, "Out of the mouth of babes" (Psalm 8:2).

My angel Avery is telling me to quiet down and tune in to the advice of our omnipotent Caregiver. So, I listen to her poignant advice and then listen to my heart. I hold still. I focus inward. The panic sweeps away. I feel calm. I feel assurance. Eli is fine. He hadn't popped pills into his mouth. I know it with surety. I know it because of the absolutely amazing companionship of the Holy Ghost.

With the almost-crisis over, I sit staring into Avery's pure eyes; her words continue ringing in my head. She instinctively knew to listen for the Holy Ghost after a prayer. I think she's really listening and absorbing what's being taught during Primary, family scripture study, and family home evenings—more deeply than I am!

One word most impressed me in her question. She personalized the gift of the Holy Ghost when she asked, "What is *your* Holy Spirit telling you?" She may not have realized how insightful her tender reminder to me was, but it certainly penetrated my soul.

The Holy Ghost can be *my* constant companion. It's pretty humbling, comforting, and motivating to contemplate that a member of the Godhead can be my own constant companion.

"He knows our thoughts and the intents of our hearts. The Holy Ghost loves us and wants us to be happy" (Craig C. Christensen, "An Unspeakable Gift from God," *Ensign*, November 2012, 12). I remember hearing Elder Craig C. Christensen teach those principles and pausing to ponder. The Holy Ghost loves me. I guess that's common sense, but never before had I given direct thought to the principle. He loves me, and He is *my* Holy Spirit—*my* companion.

My husband is my eternal companion, and even he gets tired of hearing my rambling thoughts. The Holy Spirit knows *all* of them—the pure-intentioned, the twisted, the elated, and the depressed—and He still sticks by me. He loves me constantly. What a gift. I can't think of a better gift.

Now the question is, "Does the Holy Spirit know how much *I* love Him?" The moment the question enters my mind, the Holy Spirit hears and answers. That most precious burning of the bosom that's unique to each soul, nearly indescribable, pushes its way against my ribcage and infiltrates my heart. It's a language directly communicated between His Holy Spirit and my shelled spirit. It's refreshing, calming, exhilarating, and promising all at once.

I hope Avery recognizes *her* Holy Spirit. Her astute observation from moments before still has me floored, in awe, just like the scripture says: "Little children do have words given unto them many times, which confound the wise and the learned" (Alma 32:23).

I don't classify myself as learned or wise, but I felt confounded by the words of my little one. It's no wonder that prophetic, latter-day revelation advises parents and teachers to "learn to listen, then listen to learn from children" (Russell M. Nelson, "Listen to Learn," *Ensign*, May 1991, 22).

I obviously have much to learn from my little ones. It's remarkable to think that Heavenly Father extends His partnership with me and my husband, as earthly parents, to care for valiant spirits who have been reserved for this day, who have been deemed the "chosen generation" (Gordon B. Hinckley, "Words of the Prophet: A Chosen Generation," *New Era*, January 1999, 4).

These noble souls lived in such an outstanding way during the premortal existence that they were selected and saved for this time to help prepare the world for the Second Coming. I have no doubt that my children's preparation responsibilities begin in my individual world—the world sitting smack dab in the middle of our humble home. I have no doubt that these immediate family members of the chosen generation have been sent to prepare me.

"And a little child shall lead them" (Isaiah 11:6).

I grab my notebook to try and solidify the insights my Heavenly Father gave me during these last few minutes. I write, *"Always* have medication locked away in child-resistant packaging," *"My* Holy Spirit," and "As I feel overwhelmed tending to wee hands and small demands, remember He sent these little ones to prepare me, just as much as I am to prepare them. Our symbiotic relationship is necessary for us to enter the celestial kingdom as a family unit; therefore, I need to benefit from their insights—and the only way to do that is to listen."

YOUR TURN!

What is *your* Holy Ghost telling you? It's essential to recognize the Spirit's unique way of communicating with your soul. How would you describe the way you feel and hear the Spirit's promptings? Make a list of times in your life when you've surely felt or heard the Holy Ghost. Note how the Spirit's communication style or your receptive feelings change with the type of message given (like a warning versus a prompting). Staying alert and consciously aware of how you feel and receive His messages will allow heavenly communication to come through even more clearly. Next, share what you've learned with your loved ones and ask them how they feel and hear the Holy Spirit.

Solidifying a spider's web. Reading ahead in one of our homeschool science books, I learn that a spider's web begins as a liquid and only solidifies when air touches it. Incredible! Divine details: Our faith begins as a tender form of hope; then when we have spiritual experiences, we are touched by the Holy Ghost and our hope solidifies into a testimony.

Tall or small, trees tell all. On our walk earlier today, great green pines surrounded our every step along the cleared path. Sunrays glazed their tops, but shade blanketed where we walked. I craned my neck way back to view their undersides and admire the branches' elaborate netting. Their thick trunks stood unyielding and straight like nature's wisest friends; their tops scraped skies and reached dreams. I stood so small in their presence.

I took a gander at the small one attached to my hand. "Hey, Avery, do the trees make you feel small? They do for me." She continued her skip-hop-walk and without missing a beat replied, "I always feel small." She didn't sound the least bit sad or sorry for feeling small. Her sweet voice held a matter-of-fact tone and her eyes appeared as intelligent as the trees.

Now, as I drive below tall pines and near old oaks, I wonder if that's a vital source to a child's perfection. Children experience constant reminders of their smallness. They know they depend on and have faith in bigger people. The trees and the wee ones beneath them remind me in another way of Christ's command to become as little children (see Matthew 18:3).

CHAPTER 10

A Field Trip to Remember

3:00 p.m.

Feeling rejuvenated after naptime and relieved after our mini-almost-crisis, we devour a snack and venture out the door. Recently, my first-grader, my preschooler, my peewee, and I have been busy studying about Christ's earthly ministry in preparation for Easter. We've thoughtfully examined artwork, read books and poems, sang Primary songs, and watched videos. Today's field trip aims to be a cultivating and culminating event. In our study, Christ has often been referred to as the Good Shepherd. The term piqued my pupils' interest, so I thought we'd check out a local flock of sheep to discover why sheep need a shepherd, how we are similar to sheep, and why Christ is referred to as our Shepherd.

In my head, I fully anticipate a perfectly precious teaching moment—full of spiritual symbolism and divine details. We'll stand in front of the blue-sky backdrop, near the bottom of grassy green hills, pointing at white fluffy sheep. I even pack my camera to capture the predicted picturesque moment.

I have driven by such a "backdrop" on the back roads from my parents' suburbia home. Although I have never met the owners, I hope they will welcome some gazers to admire their flock for a few minutes. Turns out, I'm right.

As I pull up the long driveway, an older gentleman approaches us. Now, I don't know much about farming, but he looks exactly like the farmers portrayed in picture books and movies—donning heavy denim pants, durable boots, and a checkered shirt that stays right in place under his charming red suspenders. He greets us with a wide grin and pure country hospitality. When he asks how he can help, I request a closer look at his sheep for me and my crew. He nods and even offers to open the first gate to the corral so we can get a closer view. My mind rejoices, "Everything is working out so well!"

The corral gate squeaks open to reveal a floor of mud three inches deep—and it smells. Now really, what was I expecting? A pristine yellow-brick road leading to the herd? I grin, square my shoulders, swoop up Eli, and advise the girls to watch their step.

We approach the inner fence and spot a dozen sheep, not quite white or fluffy, like they appear from the road—more like gray and filthy. A few sheep "baaa" in our direction, causing Anna to cling onto my leg with a velociraptor-like grip. Eli begins to whine. Avery crinkles her nose. My city-slicker family doesn't find the sight, sound, or smell soothing. Farmer Brown (we'll just call him that) stands nearby, gawking at us city folk as if *we* were the animals on parade.

I beg Avery and Anna to pose near the fence so I can snap their photo with the sheep in the background. No way. A conversation about our Savior? Not happening. All they want to do is get out of there.

As we backpedal toward the concrete, the inevitable happens: Anna slides into a mound of fly-infested sheep poop. Now, I'm a bit of a germ freak. People's germs disgust me, and animals' germs are worse. The sheep feces contaminating her new Mary Janes sends my germ-phobia alert into a code red, sirens screaming. (In hindsight, it's embarrassing, but it's really how I felt.)

I remind myself that shoes are salvageable and that I have a trusty travel-sized hand sanitizer in the minivan's glove box. By the time we actually make it across the corral, Anna slips and slides across several more sheep pies, and I feel 100 percent done with our farmland fun. I sit Anna on the curb to await my return while Avery buckles in and I strap Eli into his giant throne of a car seat. Armed with a case of baby wipes and hand sanitizer, I walk back to my small fry sitting still on the street curb, and I can't help but notice the sheepish grin between her French-braided pigtails.

To my horror, the muck multiplied. Anna's fingers are a stained giveaway brown. Artistic swipes of finger-painted fertilizer coiled like vines stretch up her legs and elbows and onto her clothes. I fling open the wipes case to reveal only two wipes left. That figures. I look up. I look around. Farmer Brown can no longer be seen. I am alone, and I can't decide if I'd rather cry or gag.

That's when the cell phone in my back pocket rings. It's my mom. My low-toned "Hello" receives an immediate, "What's wrong?"

"Sheep poop."

She wants details.

"Sheep poop everywhere."

I follow up with a brief description of the predicament while Anna's thick lashes flap up and down on those big, staring baby blues. She doesn't move a tiny muscle.

A piece of my mother's wisdom breaks through the seven-mile stare: "These are the sort of experiences she'll remember," my mom says. "Take a deep breath and then laugh about it. Call me back after you get cleaned up and tell me how it went."

I decide it is worth a try. We hang up, I take a deep breath, and I force a laugh. More like a chuckle. It feels surprisingly good. I laugh a bit more, with a smidgen of sincerity this time. Anna's eyes widen further.

"Mom, what's funny?"

"You're covered in sheep poop!"

We both giggle. Our giggles gurgle over into layers of laughter. We bubble up and overflow in belly-jiggling jolly. This was the picturesque *mom*ent. We sit on that curb with the blue-sky backdrop, the crackled old fence, the green rolling hills, and the sheep still baa-ing, and we throw our heads back and allow joy to overcome.

I get her clean to the best of our two wipes' capabilities, strip her down, bag the clothes and shoes in the trunk, and load her and her pungent stench of sheep into her car seat.

We dial Grandma and put her on speakerphone.

"Grandma? I stepped in sheep poop and got it all over me! It's *so* funny!" Anna announces, proudly.

But I think Grandma feels even more pleased.

I feel happy too. Anna could have remembered that day as the day she accidentally stepped in dung and Mom got mad. Instead, she'll remember the laughter and maybe have a mental snapshot of an understanding mother. As she gets older, I hope she'll be able to pull spiritual lessons from the event, like the fact that when mortal beings step into heaps of something we shouldn't (and we all do it), we needn't feel alone. Heavenly Father is always just a conversation away. When we explain to Him in prayer the predicament we've gotten ourselves into, our all-knowing Heavenly Father can send the Holy Spirit to whisper clues of how to remedy the mess while maintaining a smile. He wants us to smile and to laugh. He wants us to be happy—even in the hard happenings. After all, "men are, that they might have joy" (2 Nephi 2:25).

When I think of living examples of laughing and loving through the travails and tipsy turns of life, I think of my friend Jessica Wilde. Right now she's living in limbo, moving from Iowa to North Carolina and waiting for their house purchase to close. For the past two months, the Wilde family has called a hotel home—that's two adults, six kids (ten years and younger), one cat, and one guinea pig squished into one hotel room. Jessica tells me that hotel living means daily grocery shopping, because the mini fridge barely holds a gallon of milk and a few essentials. It means frequent trips to the laundromat, with arms full of kiddos and overflowing laundry baskets. It also means constant noise control duty, in attempts to not bother the people above, below, and on each side of their room. And it means feeling embarrassed about how many times they've set off the hotel fire alarm. Sadly, she's also learned that in such close quarters, hotel living means that when the stomach flu strikes one child, it quickly takes down the whole family. At one point, the toilet, garbage cans, and sink were all being used simultaneously. It wasn't their fondest family moment.

Yet, to my amazement, she shares her stories with a widespread smile and infectious laugh. Her comments don't come across as complaints, but as twists and turns in the story of her life—ones she approaches with ready hands and a happy heart. Since she had her first child, her motto has been, "Don't get mad; get the camera!" She believes that the challenges we face now often become the best stories to recall later in life.

Most inspiring of all is her perspective. She readily recognizes that hotel living is quite plush accommodations, considering the destitute living situations of so many children of God. Plus, this year her family has faced a serious and rare illness in her youngest son, and because of that, she says she's able to more clearly define what is and what is not deemed a significant trial. Compared with the illness of her son, she says hotel living is simply laughable.

I want to identify the little laughable things too (even when they don't feel little). I want to look at the good and the bad with trust that it will all work out. I want to trust enough that I can laugh and make memories along the bumpy, dirty, and some-times-painful day.

"The only way to get through life is to laugh your way through it," said Marjorie Hinckley (*Small and Simple Things* [Salt Lake City: Deseret Book, 2003], 126).

So I set a goal for more giggles. I'm hoping that my initial forced giggles will eventually transform and bubble into those deep, hearty laughs that echo across the air. I love those laughs—they're usually better than the joke itself! Laughter sounds delightful, feels delightful, and spreads delight. And everyone could benefit from a triple scoop of delight each day!

The scriptures tell us, "Men are, that they might have joy" (2 Nephi 2:25), and President Boyd K. Packer counseled us to, "Find happiness in ordinary things, and keep your sense of humor" (Boyd K. Packer, "Do Not Fear," *Ensign*, May 2004). I love that!

My trusty spiral notebook returns to my hand, and I note, "My picturesque **mom**ents will look different than His—laugh and love it! Find delight in the divine details."

YOUR TURN!

Want to focus more on joy or add more laughter to life? Reread Elder Joseph B. Wirthlin's conference talk "Come What May, and Love It" (*Ensign*, November 2008, 26–28) and "If We Can Laugh at It, We Can Live with It" by Brad Wilcox (*Ensign*, March 2000). Then purposefully practice giving in to the giggles. It'll be fun!

Gotcha at the crossroads. I add the sheep-poop clothes to a few dirty items from my kiddos' perpetually full clothes hamper and load them all into the washing machine for yet another round of laundry. As the rainbow of clothes waterfall from the laundry bag I spot a half-filled green balloon from our favorite restaurant. "Gotcha!" I yank it out. More "gotchas" follow as I captured trailing tissues and a purple princess lip gloss.

I learned the importance of being at the laundry's crossroads early in my children's lives. Once, a soiled diaper snuck into the washing machine. It swelled with water, more than doubling its size, inflating until plastic crystals wilted away and cloaked the clothes like a snow flurry. To think of the dirty diaper's remnants swirling around, blending with soapsuds and clothing, completely grossed me out—and the green peas that survived the cycle confirmed my disgust.

No wonder I've been advised to be at the crossroads of my children's lives—snatching out Satan as I spot his sneaky ways and suggesting extra stain remover as necessary. As my beginners decide which pathway to pursue, I have the responsibility to counsel them at the forks in their paths. Sometimes, as their stable guide I comfort and assure, "This too shall pass." And sometimes I'm called upon to sternly warn, "Do *not* pass—make a better choice."

President Thomas S. Monson said, "The shifting sands of popular opinion, the power of the peer group, in all too many instances become an irresistible magnet drawing downward to destruction the precious sons and daughters of God. We become the stable force, the port of safety in the

storm-tossed seas, the watchman on the tower, even
the guide at the crossroads" (Thomas S. Monson,
"Building Bridges," *New Era*, November 1985).

CHAPTER 11

Open the Book to Cook

4:00 p.m.

can feel it coming. A child will soon ask the dreaded question—the one I face daily but rarely know the answer to: "What's for dinner?" When my husband picked me as his lucky eternal lady, let's just say it wasn't because of my kitchen skills. I'm a sweet tooth but no foodie. I don't *love* my food. Don't get me wrong; I eat—to survive. But I just don't salivate and stew over it, and I definitely don't want to waste valuable time on it. But as a mama bird of three small chicks whose beaks never stop chirping for more worms, I'm always in the kitchen, regardless of my low pain tolerance for kitchen duty.

Knowing the inevitable "What's for dinner?" question is moments away, I try to proactively seek inspiration. Elevating to tiptoes, I stretch for the cupboard filled with sundry idle cookbooks. And with that gentle upwards movement, the inspiration starts to come down—but not in regards to food. An image of a teetering teenager from my congregation floods my mind.

For the past six months I've served as the leader of the young ladies in our ward. It's been a steep learning curve, but I'm beginning to feel more secure in my call (though I still freeze statuesquely when the bishop calls me "President Poe"). As part of getting to know the girls, I'm in the midst of conducting one-on-one interviews with them. So far, these interviews have proven to be incredibly revealing; I get the scoop on their spiritual habits and usually learn a bit about their personal lives as well. I notice that my love for them grows as I get to know their quirks, challenges, talents, and souls a bit better—no wonder my husband loves to conduct "personal interviews" with the kiddos on a regular basis.

As I grip the attained cookbook in my hands, my mind flashes back to a visit made last Sunday. I stopped to say howdy at the home of a spunky and beautiful young woman since she was a no-show at church (and I worry about her constantly). Still in sloppy pajamas, she politely led me to her father's office. She offered me a plump leather chair, and I felt unusually presidential smiling at her from behind the grand desk.

After rattling off a few standard icebreaker questions— "How's school?" and "What have you been up to lately?"—we said an opening prayer and dove in. I asked how her personal prayers were. She said she had said one last night and that it had been one of the first times in a long time. *Eeek*—that's great news!

"How did it go?" I asked (probably too energetically).

"Fine," she replied, and then added coolly, "I asked if the Church is true."

I was on the edge of my seat. "And?" was all that squeaked out.

"I don't know. I didn't get an answer."

I slid back into the grooves of the plush leather. I didn't know what to say yet, so I listened for more.

"I wish I could just know," she said.

There she sat, with the Book of Mormon and Holy Bible closed in front of her. And there she sat, wishing to know truth.

Standing in the kitchen, holding that cookbook in my hands and replaying the experience in my mind, I held an "I should have said" mock conversation in my mind. Relying on my novice spiritual symbolism skills, I conjure up this wishful dialogue between my cloudy-minded young woman and her green leader.

I should have reeled her in with, "I knew a girl once who wanted to learn how to cook. I ran into her at a bookstore a while back. She walked up to me, clutching a copy of my all-time favorite cookbook and said, 'I really wish I knew how to cook.' Then she placed my favorite cookbook on a nearby shelf, shrugged her shoulders, and walked away. Can you guess what I did?"

This is where my sweet young woman would indifferently say, "You told her she should read the cookbook."

And I'd say, "Exactly! I ran after her and told her that I knew this cookbook was superb—I had made nearly every recipe in the book, and though challenging, they weren't too difficult to follow and the food turned out absolutely delectable. I suggested she read it, and even offered to let her borrow my own copy. She agreed. So I dropped my cookbook off at her house that night, and over the next little while she diligently read it from cover to cover."

At this point, my young woman would feel engaged in the story. She'd say, "What happened next, Sister Poe?" (In this mock conversation, my teenager is totally enthused by my storytelling!)

I'd continue, "She came over to my house one day to return the cookbook, and she said, 'It was a nice read and the pictures of the food look delicious, but I still don't know how to cook.' Can you believe that?"

By now, a smile would be plastered from ear to ear and my young woman would have received and understood the message. But since I don't stop talking all that easily, I'd have to finish:

"You know what I did? I threw my hands in the air and told her she had to get her booty in the kitchen, mix up some ingredients, and actually give it a try. Now, my sweet young woman, I know the Holy Bible and the Book of Mormon are true. I've tried out the principles and commandments given in it, and the blessings are spiritually delicious. I know if you read it, pray about it, and try to live by its teachings, you too will know if the Church is true."

I'd then share with her John 7:17, which reads, "If any man will *do* his will, he shall know of the doctrine, whether it be of God, or whether I speak of myself" (emphasis added). I wouldn't want her to just believe the words I'm speaking—because my words cannot settle a soul; that's the Spirit's gift. We each must learn for ourselves what is right and true and good, and this scripture describes how to go about that. Note that the word *do* is purposefully placed before *know*, for we must *do* to know. It takes great faith to do something before knowing if it's going to work or if it's worthwhile. But by showing a humble and willing speck of faith, we grow our faith. It's a miraculous and divinely designed process.

At this point, my inspired and committed young woman would then reach across the desk, give me a hug, and say, "Thanks, Sister Poe. I'll read the scriptures, and then I'll actually give living the gospel a try." Right? I'm just sure this conversation could have done some good!

Oh, why didn't I say all that? Thinking about it over and over again, I know it would have been perfect! Maybe it would have changed her—I know she has changed me. And truth be told, I know that girl lives inside me too. I think she's within all of us. I feel her when my questions seem beyond my capacity, and I wish someone would just hand me the answer. Deep down I know I need to pray more and talk less. I know I need to trust more and worry less. I know I need to seek Him—and seeking takes time, effort, and heart. But when I'm tired, confused, and flustered, I just want to know *now*. Here's the thing, though: on the heavy-weight questions—the ones that can transform lives here and through eternity—it doesn't matter how many people hand me the answer. None of their answers matter. Only the all-knowing, all-loving, perfect One can provide the answer to settle my soul. He sends the answer, and He is the answer. Maybe *that* is what I really need to say to that girl, and to that girl within me.

Setting down the cookbook, I resolve to pick up the phone and continue the conversation, or perhaps write her a note. Call me a traditionalist, but something magical can happen when carefully selected handwritten words encounter a disheartened heart.

In fact, I was the receiver of such a note just yesterday. It had been "one of those days." Everywhere I turned, a mess needed cleaning. A fruit smoothie splattered against a wall, a dresser received graffiti-like scrawls, and clutter spilled out of every corner. Plus, the lost hours of sleep from the night before transformed my six-year-old's cognitive ability into a four-year-old's, my four-year-old's thought process decomposed into a fourteen-month-old's, and my fourteen-month-old's reversed into an infant's. Or so I thought.

After a rocky first half of the day, Avery handed me a colorful homemade construction-paper card. Written in her best handwriting and adorned with stickers, it read, "Thank you for beeing my mom." Even more touching, the inside read, "I thenk you giv us happy thots and that you are a good part of are family."

Her sprawled out letters stretched right into my heart. I instantaneously realized I had allowed short-fused feelings to rule many moments of my day. Mental replays from a few particular communications exposed one-sided commands and instructions. I reviewed the last few hours and asked myself some serious questions: Had I hugged her? Had we had a one-on-one conversation? Had we laughed together? Had I told her how much I adore her, or how proud I am of the girl she's becoming? Sadly, no. My answer to each question was no. And how did my little girl respond to her blundering mother?

Take note of this: Her cue did not surface in the form of, "Hey, mom, you're really cranky today. Will you please be nice?" Nope. Instead, my precious angel said thank you. Her handwritten note spun my attitude right around. As if a fairy godmother waved her wand and a magical ding sounded in the air, Mad Mama went packing and Mild Mom finished the day.

What melts a heart? Or better yet, *who* melts the heart? Only the Holy Spirit can. But I must let Him in. The bottom line is, if I hadn't opened the card, the day would have continued as it started. And if my young woman never opens her scriptures, her testimony will never grow.

The scriptures say, "His anger is not turned away, but his hand is stretched out still" (2 Nephi 19:8). What a visual scripture. I can see His hand stretching toward me. No matter how bad the day, or how tough the trial, His hand is stretched out still. But am I stretching my hand toward His in return?

I've learned a bit more about this principle during the past few years as I've studied scripture stories involving rocks. I've come to love the solid symbolism packed into the naturally occurring beauties. For example, Christ extended his hand and touched the clear stones prepared by the brother of Jared, providing light during the long voyage to the unknown promised land (Ether

2–3). When the wandering Israelites became thirsty, the Lord instructed Moses to strike a rock and bring forth water (Exodus 17). And when the young and faithful David faced a seemingly invincible giant, he launched a smooth stone (1 Samuel 17). Truly, the Lord prepares rock-hard solutions for rock-hard problems.

But just as I must extend my hand to reach His outstretched one, I must also accept the rocks He prepares and then use them. David's stone would have no effect if he had no courage to sling them toward the gigantic Goliath. The Israelites would have become dehydrated had Moses not listened and obeyed the prompting to hit a rock with a stick. And the clear stones used by the brother of Jared would have remained clear stones if he had not faith to ask the Lord to light them.

If I hadn't opened, read, and applied the teachings from my daughter's grateful love note, then my afternoon would have mirrored my morning. And as long as my young woman ignores the Book of Mormon, Holy Bible, and gospel principles, her testimony will remain lifeless. I'm beginning to see that this quest for spiritual lessons amongst my daily life is also a rock, prepared for me as a personal rock-hard solution. As I lift it, I'm feeling more capable of elevating from mommy survival mode to thrive mode.

I tack, "Learn to cook; open the book. Use the rocks God gave us," onto my day's growing list of spiritual symbols.

YOUR TURN!

Who do you know who *needs* a thank-you note? Commit to writing at least one person a note this week. Include words describing the good you see in that person (practice telling yourself a story, if necessary). For an extra challenge, refer to a spiritual symbol or moment in your message.

What "rocks" has Heavenly Father prepared especially for you and your trials? Are there any that remain untouched or underutilized? Or maybe you're in desperate need of a "rock" and can't find one? Pray to find your rocks and to know how and when to use them. There is a plan prepared!

Enjoy. "Mom, can we have a vitamin?" "I need a drink." "Is there more smoothie?" "Where's a napkin?" "Will you spread peanut butter on it?"

The questions fire in succession rapidly. It's a relentless Q&A foodie session.

And then comes the kicker: "What can I have after I eat this?" The plate is full. I have just prepared a well-balanced, fresh meal. Their needs are met. And they already want what's next.

"Enjoy what you have! Can't you just be thankful and enjoy before you ask for more?" I sputter.

And as the agitated syllables escape my lips, I feel Him. He's smiling and nodding His head in agreement—*at me*. After a weekend's worth of relentless "help me" prayers have babbled from my mind toward heaven, He's saying, "Yes! That's it. Listen to your words." So I do. They tumble and turn over and over again like clothes in the dryer: "Can't you just be thankful and enjoy before you ask for more?"

I want to crumble to the floor. I'm full of ingratitude. I'm always wanting more—more than I need, more than I deserve—and for selfish reasons. Why can't I just be thankful and enjoy the countless blessings and glory all around me before asking for more?

It's time to leave behind my relentless concerns about what's next. Good-bye, "what if"s and "why not"s. Farewell, "if only" and "but please." Wave away worries and welcome what He's already done.

I want to thank Him for bubbles in the puddle, for mile-high stacks of stuffed animals, for crayon love notes, and for rich soil etched into the bottom of rain boots. It's time to notice little things with a big, grateful heart.

Keep it on the table. At dinner I overhear Anna explain the goodness of ketchup to her older sister, but Avery isn't convinced. Anna's final analysis is, "Well, it's yummy to me, but yucky to you."

Right now one child won't eat meat, one refuses melted cheese (which means no grilled cheese sandwiches, quesadillas, or pizza!), and one doesn't do noodles or soup. What one mouth adores another mouth spits out. With all of our quirks, immature taste buds, and resistance to new flavors, putting together a menu that all five family members will consume (and vote yummy versus yucky) is like putting together a thousand-piece jigsaw puzzle of a golf ball.

As chief chef of the Poe home, I know I need to continue offering a variety of entrées and appetizers so their repertoire of food choices will eventually expand. I try to convince the kids by saying, "I know you didn't like it last time, but take a bite and maybe you'll like it this time." I'll be honest, usually they still don't like it. But once in a while their eyes get big and they announce, "I liked it this time!" Oh the joy!

Divine details: The role of chief chef can be relatable to the role of member missionary. I must continue offering gospel principles and urging others to just try it at this time in their lives. Over time, taste buds for spiritual nourishment can mature. Perhaps one of these days or decades, a fellow man or woman will take the bite, their eyes will get big as their spirit enlarges, and they will like it. In fact, they'll love it and will do anything to get more of that delicious, eternally nourishing food. It's up to me to keep it on the table.

CHAPTER 12

It's Raining—It's Pouring

While the oven crisps my homemade mac-n-cheese, I painstakingly cut intricate chameleons out of cardstock paper in preparation for one of next week's science lessons. Meanwhile, little feet thunder across the ceiling in carefree jubilation. I long for such free play but stick to maneuvering the scissors along spiral tails. Why do I devote endless time and energy to nature studies, classic children's literature, math games, and history lessons?

I ponder that for a few minutes and decide that I'm motivated on three levels. In fact, these three levels of motivation come directly from the scriptures and can be applied to so many things mothers do in behalf of their children.

First: I believe it's the right thing to do. I have faith.

Second: I'm thinking with a futuristic perspective. I hope this extra time, effort, and attention will benefit their future.

Third: I love my kids; parenting is all about love. This one captures the lion's share of my motives. A pure parental love is unconditional, merciful, all-encompassing, and as perfect as parents on earth can get. It's the underlying reason for every day, week, month, and year.

Faith, hope, and charity correlate with much more than

Jessica Poe

homeschooling. Take food, for example. Why do I spend so much energy in the buying, prepping, cooking, baking, serving, and cleaning sequence? It's the same trio of answers. I have faith that food put into the body fosters life. I hope the food will keep my precious family members healthy and strong. But above all, it's because I love them with all my heart. Just imagining my children suffering from hunger—real hunger—whittling away to bones, crying desperately for a morsel of food. . . . The pretend vision pulls my heartstrings.

The same three answers align with why I remain true to my testimony. I have faith in Heavenly Father and His Son, Jesus Christ. I hope for life eternal with God, Christ, and my family. Above all, I have felt the purest form of charity from Heavenly Father, from His Son, Jesus Christ, and from the Holy Ghost, and I feel a reciprocating love and charity for Them.

"Wherefore, there must be faith; and if there must be faith there must also be hope; and if there must be hope there must also be charity" (Moroni 10:20).

I write down, "Faith, hope, and charity—the answer to 'Why?'" in my spiral notebook, and then glance at the clock. Oh no, the dreaded five o'clock hour rapidly approaches! When the clock strikes five, my little ones transform into needy, pouty, and even screaming banshees. Here's my theory: As evening approaches, the energy revived from the afternoon nap depletes and all toys lose appeal thanks to quaking tummies. Throw in the anticipation of Daddy's homecoming, and their little brains and bodies nearly combust. It's painful to the ears and makes my circuits short-circuit. For all involved, it's a lethal combination.

Tonight needs to be different. I grasp for strategic defense just as impending squabbles gurgle and the house begins to stir. It still sounds muffled in the background, like the grumblings of the dark clouds outside, but it's definitely in forward motion. I don't have much time now. Here's an idea: I'll host a dance party while I finish up dinner preparations. Perhaps the newness of an up-tempo beat could create an entertaining diversion. I pop in some tunes I've never listened to before and push play—just as my phone chimes its familiar piano riff.

84

Our "hellos" are barely audible. Blaring trumpets, banging drums, and screeching children blast the airwaves. It sounds like an out-of-tune elementary school's band practice! My mom hears an amplified version of the chaos thanks to her headset; so I apologize and begin excusing myself from the phone conversation when my husband walks through the front door. Surprise! He's early, and he's soaked. Looks like the rain clouds let loose all at once.

It happened so fast! And it all added up to such a maddening mess! From his point of view, his straggling wife, who hasn't seen a mirror in hours (let alone a makeup brush), stands chit-chatting on the phone, with kids chucking toys amidst blaring noise and an unfinished dinner. (Later that night, Alex confessed to feeling the bass and hearing the ruckus from the mailbox—that's how loud it was.)

Doesn't it often add up so quickly? How can life feel fine, even peaceful, one minute and then swallow us in sound—or even suffering—the next? This applies to so many and in a variety of ways, but especially during trials. Hard times can throw us to our knees with force and fury—and we may stay down there for a significant stretch. The old adage, "When it rains, it pours," rings true; but out of the rain, the prayers, and the piles arise empowered, precious people.

My sweet friend Shawna Wilson comes to mind. When her father was diagnosed with the swine flu back in 2009, it threw her and her family to their knees. This was no ordinary flu, even though her father had been blessed with perfectly normal health before the virus. She was pregnant at the time and not permitted to see him in such a contagious state, at least until the H1N1 virus had run its course and it was time to say good-bye. Walking into the hospital room and seeing him lying limply, lifelessly, hooked to machines, she collapsed to the floor. "How could this happen so fast?" she wondered. Just one week before, he had been fit and fine. On that chilling November day, Shawna's good-byes focused on one heartfelt plea: she begged her dying father to protect her unborn child. She felt so worried about the baby girl inside her.

Two Novembers later, that same baby girl—now blonde and bouncy—was diagnosed with an aggressive form of leukemia.

Shawna had been in Utah visiting family, and with that diagnosis, life changed dramatically. As the clouds shifted, the rains let loose. Shawna stayed in Utah so Tenley could receive care at Primary Children's Hospital. While caring for her nineteen-month-old in a furious fight for life, she simultaneously mothered her four-year-old, Taryn, and was long-distance wife to Robbie, who had to return to their home in Nevada for work. Once again she was in a familiar position: on her knees, surrounded by piles of pain and pressure.

The following six months were overwhelming. The days felt long and daunting; the nights dragged on, lonely and interrupted. Every four hours, nurses checked vitals, changed diapers, and poked and prodded her baby girl. She tried covering the sterile hospital room with layers of home: a tall lamp in the corner, a shaggy rug on the floor, pictures of loved ones on the walls, and plenty of cozy blankets. Shawna says she desperately yearned for home and normal mom life. What she would have done for a day of laundry, planning dinner, or monitoring a play date! What once was considered a burden or something that "just had to be done," she now longed for.

This "new normal" of chemotherapy, of a tiny daughter with cancer, of another young daughter traumatized from cancer in the family, of a long-distance marriage—it was so much to handle at one time. Yet Shawna says she felt her burdens lighten by the prayers of others. She also felt her father fulfilling that parting plea from two years earlier. He attended Tenley in ways Shawna couldn't. He went with Tenley through surgery, and he comforted her when her limited vocabulary couldn't explain the pains.

And then, on New Year's Day, another heavy helping piled on her plate. She was flabbergasted to find out she was pregnant—with twins. Twins. That news could be received in so many different ways. I mean, how would I have reacted in the midst of all that?

Shawna saw it as a sign from Heavenly Father that their family's cancer chapter would soon end and a new chapter of twin babies would begin. In fact, when she told her husband, Robbie, he said, "Now we have something to look forward to!" They chose anticipation of joy—of treasured twins—in the midst of trials. How beautiful and inspiring to collect treasures from trials and see the Savior's love in the storm.

So here in my trivial trial of the witching hour, I look for treasure. I want to see the divine details, and what I see is my husband's response to our imperfect storm. He doesn't judge, he doesn't complain, he doesn't balk—all of which would result in a family-sized explosion. Instead, he simply washes his hands like he does every night, wrings out his jacket, and gives me and each pint-sized person a squeeze and kiss. Then he offers to help with the dinner's final touches. Ah, thank Heavenly Father for my true helpmeet and teammate! He is a treasure, and so are the tiny tots hanging from his knees.

Modern revelation teaches us that spirits were strategically arranged in families before coming to this earth and that our treasured family units can continue after this life. So it's no coincidence that families are crucial right now, during our time in mortal existence. We know that this earthly stint is meant to stretch and strengthen us. It's meant to be hard, to rain piles of trials. But out of the rain and the piles and the prayers, we can grow into powerful, precious people—people with potential beyond what our mortal minds can comprehend. Isn't that's why we jumped for joy in the premortal existence? Isn't that why we're here now?

One of my all-time favorite quotes (one I refer to time and time again when the load feels heavy and heaped all at once) is by Elder Neal A. Maxwell:

> How can you and I really expect to glide naively through life, as if to say, "Lord, give me experience, but not grief, not sorrow, not pain, not opposition, not betrayal, and certainly not to be forsaken. Keep from me, Lord, all those experiences which made Thee what Thou art! Then let me come and dwell with Thee and fully share Thy joy!" (Neal A. Maxwell, "Lest Ye Be Wearied and Faint in Your Minds," *Ensign*, May 1991)

And so when it all adds up and pours down so fast, when we collapse to our knees and wonder if our own trials can be removed, we can think back to the three motivating factors: faith, hope, and charity.

First: We have faith that God is real, that He loves us, and that He gives all trials solely for our experience and good.

Second: We hope for, and look forward to, the time when we will unite with our elder Brother, Jesus Christ, with our spiritual Father and our eternal family.

Third (and most of all): We rely on love—the love of God given through the grace of His Son and our Savior. It's not possible without His grace.

So, I wonder, what was the spiritual lesson learned? What divine details of truth did I discover? Faith, hope, and charity can get us through the witching hour—and our darkest hours. I sprint for my pen and notepad.

YOUR TURN!

Is it raining where you are? Sprinkle or downpour? Pool those drops on paper, and then work to identify the three levels of motivation for weathering your storm: faith, hope, and charity. Seeing and understanding the "why" may provide insight for just the right "how" to weather the storm.

Even pressure. Apparently, I'm on a breaking binge. Within the last forty-eight hours I've broken my daughter's ladybug antenna headband (just minutes before her dance recital), our computer router, a dinner plate, my phone, a fishbowl, and my elbow. Okay, my elbow's not really broken, but it is still hurting two days after I accidentally collided with our freezer's ice machine (long story). So once again, I'm getting that "all at once" feeling, and when everything crashes down, it often feels like an outside source is determined to break *me*.

While pondering those thoughts, I came across another science project for homeschool. Here's what to do: Take an egg in the palm of your hand, with fingers wrapped tightly around it—now squeeze. Squeeze as hard as possible. Too scared it'll break and egg goo will drip all over? Don't be scared—Heavenly Father designed an egg's shape to be extremely durable, despite its fragile reputation. The key is to apply the pressure evenly. If pressure punctures just one spot on the egg's shell (like when whacking it against a bowl), then the yolk will surely splat. But when pressure pushes evenly, the egg remains intact.

So, Heavenly Father isn't trying to break me. Instead, He holds me in His palm, where the pressure is purposefully being applied evenly to *protect me* from breaking. Maybe I'm more durable than I give myself credit for.

CHAPTER 13

Serving Sassie

6:00 p.m.

During a recent conference at church, our chapel was adorned with fresh flowers and plants. I received an assignment, prior to the conference, to deliver a fresh plant to a woman who had been shut in her home for weeks. I was also to leave with her a spiritual thought from the conference—easy enough.

The woman assigned to me was a beloved elderly character in our ward—and I do mean character. Appropriately named Sassie, she's admired for her spunk and zeal. She uses her gregarious personality to gab about the gospel—what a talent she has!

I didn't deliver the plant directly following the conference due to schedule constraints, but glancing at the plant on my end table, I can see it needs to arrive at Sassie's house ASAP—before I officially kill it. I have a history of murdering plants, and this one already sprouts signs of sickness. So I decide to drop it off at her house before stopping by my parents' house to check on my dad, who is ill. Thankfully, my generous husband kisses me and accepts all bedtime ritual duties, and away I go.

Driving through her mobile home park, I feel an overwhelming sense of ingratitude for the blessings and good fortune I have become passive to. Once parked, I look at my watch and start my thirty-minute mental timer; I know that's awful, but I feel like I must manage my time in order to visit my parents that evening too.

Before I make it to the three ascending steps to Sassie's front door, her large silhouette pushes forward, making a grand yet graceless entrance. Luckily, she catches herself on the banister before momentum can grab hold. With gargantuan panache, she blows out an exhale, sweeps her white hair out of her eyes, and gives me an infectious smile.

"I have a visitor!" she announces to her two yapping pooches, who twist and twirl between her ankles to see who managed to get her up and out of the large chair in the corner of the room.

"Hello, Sassie! I've brought you a plant," I state the obvious as I pathetically hold out the miserable-looking greenery.

"Welcome! Welcome! Come on in!" she says as she begins the tiring trek back to her chair.

I wind my way along the narrow pathway to her living room. In every direction stacked boxes and plastic containers climb to the ceiling. Knickknacks ornament every empty space, and every-thing has a place. The thing is, there aren't many places left. She directs me toward a folding chair in the corner and catches her breath as she safely situates herself in a blanketed, oversized chair.

I've spoken with Sassie at church several times and loved her from the start. Always smiling and hugging those around her, Sassie stands out in bright-colored dresses and large prints to match her spirit and charisma. There is never a dull moment with her around.

"Want to know my favorite Bible hero?" she asks with a spar-kle in her eye.

"Yes."

"John the Baptist."

I take the bait. "Why John?"

"Because he lost his head for the gospel," she wheezes and cackles straight from her heart.

"But really," she continues, "he is my favorite. I hope when I get to heaven, I can marry him. I love him."

She's serious. She then rattles off bookloads of interesting facts about John the Baptist, his father, Zacharias, and his mother, Elizabeth. She concludes with, "And another reason John's my favorite? He was wild—just like me!" The corners of her mouth quiver with joy as her white eyebrows wiggle up and down, and she pulls on straggling white hairs from the side of her head to make them stand up straight.

I really do hope she'll get to marry John the Baptist (or another worthy man) in the next life, because she deserves a noble and grand mate. She has lived in especially difficult circumstances since the beginning of her earthly life. Her birth father and mother didn't welcome her like the royal and loyal spirit she is. As young, runaway teenagers, they were ill equipped to care for a child. Instead, they frantically wrapped her newborn body in newspaper and placed her in the bottom of a trashcan. Nearby neighbors heard her cry and delivered her to a hospital, where she was properly identified. Thankfully, her maternal grandmother was notified, and the elderly woman stuck by the babe, raising her with wit and charm.

To that rough beginning, Sassie simply smiles and says, "In the beginning when spirits received assignments, someone asked, 'Who will take this one?' But no one raised their hand. So I said, 'I'll take it. I'll try.'" And she tries with all her might.

A moment displaying her constant efforts occurred one day as an adult when Sassie traveled in the backseat of a van next to her best friend's sixteen-month-old son. Her best friend sat in the passenger seat, and the father of that family sped along the road. A fast slam on the brakes spun the car sideways and into a large truck. During the spin, Sassie pulled herself up and over the helpless child, burying his head into her armpit. The gutsy move saved his life, but the impact broke Sassie's neck and fractured her jaw in multiple places.

Today she sits in her chair, with ailments related to that crash from more than twenty years ago. She doesn't complain but graphically explains in a matter-of-fact manner what's going on with her physical body.

I listen as she testifies and teaches me for nearly an hour. She perches like a wise white owl with regality, and I, the beggar chick at her feet. She speaks of enduring to the end, tells stories of times she felt served and loved, and relays things she's learned from her scripture study.

Finally, I muster up the courage to tell her I need to leave, even though I would love to listen more. She nods understandingly. My eyes brim with tears because I feel dreadful leaving her alone, in pain and in her chair—but she'd never have me feel sorry for her. She simply says, "Hogwash," waves her hand at me to dismiss those tears at once, and changes the subject.

Though I'm here to give her a plant, she insists on giving goodies to my little ones. She reveals yellow bunny purses with packages of fruit snacks inside for my girls. For Eli, she seizes a miniature balloon on a stick poking out of an empty vase. In exchange, she accepts the limp plant and places it on a tiny windowsill above the kitchen sink.

As she gathers the trinkets and introduces the plant to its new habitat, I feel prompted to leave her with a prayer.

We humbly bow our heads, and a grand and awe-inspiring feeling of love for her fills my heart. I thank Heavenly Father for Sassie's strength and testimony, her missionary work, and her example. I also pray for her with fervor that she'll be watched over and comforted, that her body will feel little pain, and that her spirit will continue to soar. Throughout the pleadings I hear Sassie whisper small sounds of agreement or gratitude to her Heavenly Father. When I can't think of the right word, she fills in my blank. We truly pray with unity of heart and mind in a way I haven't before. The prayer comes from two individuals but is knit together with one love. It feels like what Alma commanded of his new converts at the waters of Mormon:

"And he commanded them that there should be no contention one with another, but that they should look forward with one eye, having one faith and one baptism, having their hearts knit together in unity and in love one towards another" (Mosiah 18:21).

With an amen, we lift our heads and I rush to hug her in her chair. She gazes up and sees a small square plaque resting on a full shelf. She wants me to have it. Now, I already have an arm full of gifts for my kiddos, and I just can't take another one of her personal items, but she is adamant. The white tile balances on a black stand and reads, "Charity never faileth"—the perfect lesson.

During my drive away, I search for symbolism from within that small service. My mind reels as I dissect. I went to serve but left being served. I went to uplift but left lifted beyond anything I could have anticipated. I went to share a spiritual message, but she gave the spiritual message to me. I went to show love but left feeling loved.

"How did she do that?" I think to myself.

And the Spirit repeats the answer, "Charity never faileth."

Sassie oozes with charity—it fills her soul and overflows, dripping spiritual life particles onto all who come near. Because of her matured love of Christ, she spreads that love to souls she comes in contact with *and* she feels intensely and eternally loved herself. It's a magical equation.

Truly, charity can never fail because it's always working double duty. The more one soul loves another, the more that same soul feels love in return. The more I attempt to serve, the more the Spirit serves me with love. It's as inseparable as inhaling and exhaling. Spirit in, Spirit out. Service in, service out.

President Gordon B. Hinckley said, "The best antidote I know for worry is work. The best medicine for despair is service. The best cure for weariness is the challenge of helping someone who is even more tired" ("Words of the Prophet: Put Your Shoulder to the Wheel," *New Era*, July 2000, 4).

No wonder I left her house with double the gifts and love I gave. "To serve or be served, that is the answer. Charity never faileth," I jot in my notebook.

YOUR TURN!

Think of an individual you know who serves as a living example of charity. Really pause and pick a person.

Why did you think of *that* person? What admirable traits or specific examples come to mind about that person? What lessons can you learn from him or her that can apply in your life?

With those answers in mind, set a specific goal relating to charity and service. Make it a goal for today and for the week. Record your thoughts and feelings at the end of each day of the week.

Handmade and heartfelt. "Look, Mom! Look what I made! I'm going to give it to Grandma. She's going to really like it!" Anna's smooth milky hands hold up a drawing of a pig prancing next to a bowed ballerina and a red rocket blazing across the sky. Her big sister barrels down the hallway with a beaded bracelet in a candy cane pattern—another gift for Grandma. Even Eli has a present in mind. "Me too! Me too! For Grandma!" he proudly proclaims as he hands a scribbled paper my way. Looking closely, I spy a few wavy circles corresponding with his description: "Balloons!" I love how little children can enthusiastically create homemade gifts and feel so confident in their masterpieces.

I've seen many adults asked to produce a handmade gift, and they stew over what to construct, feeling uncomfortable and unworthy of the task. Throughout the creative process, pent up self-doubt brims as the gift undergoes thorough scrutiny. Even the presentation of the gift can feel torturous and awkward. Many times the first words from the adult creator only describe their mistakes to the receiver.

On the other hand, little children beam with pride. They can't wait for their gift to be unwrapped, and then they explode with an "I made that!" Theirs is a perfect pride—not the kind of pride that destroys souls but the kind that uplifts and motivates everyone around them. Heavenly Father gave a similar example of perfect pride in the first chapter of our standard works. When He created the earth, He looked over His handiwork and declared it a success: "And God saw every thing that He had made, and, behold, it was very good"

(Genesis 1:31). Note that it wasn't "kind of good" or "all right, except for that bunch of trees over there"—but "very good." I love that!

Lesson learned: no excuses, just take perfect pride in your handiwork—whatever it may be.

CHAPTER 14

The Man in the Moon

7:00 p.m.

I leave Sassie's feeling spiritually uplifted and restored, but as soon as I arrive at my parents' house, I subsequently feel sucker punched by mortal reality. As I enter the house, I find my dad in excruciating pain. He has terminal thyroid cancer. The doctors have appeased our family by reporting that thyroid cancer is the best cancer to get, but is any cancer *good* to get? It's still cancer, and it's still spreading—though slowly, buying us more time to learn from him. Trial medications and treatments have aided his battle but are also to blame for myriad vicious ailments. Today his body is suffering uncommon side effects from what was supposed to be a routine procedure. And the prescribed pain medication to counteract the side effects poisons his body.

Now, his heavy chest smashes against his lungs, resulting in short, shallow breaths. His legs and arms jolt in spasms, his stomach lurches and heaves, and a dense fog has settled over his mind.

My mom deserves a breath of crisp night air and needs a few items from the store, so she steps out while I temporarily step in. Dad lays sprawled in bed, twitching from one position to the next in search of relief. I watch him sit up and punch the air and then lie down and kick his legs. He groans and moans, twists and turns. This is not like my dad.

My dad is a superhero. Ask him how he's feeling and he'll flex his biceps, grin, and say, "Life is good." He doesn't call in sick, even when he should. He resists reporting new symptoms when I think physicians need an update. He just keeps smiling and keeps going. He's a fabulously stubborn, full-of-life servant of the Lord in my mind. He's my unbreakable superhero—but at the moment, he looks pretty broken.

There's a reason for the term "fighting cancer." My dad looks and feels like he is in the midst of a losing battle. Though the lines on his face appear tired and old, he also seems as helpless as one of my babes. Witnessing his physical pain feels painful to me. I don't know how my mom does it day in and day out.

I ask if I can say a prayer, and he agrees. Afterward, he curls up in the fetal position and allows me to stroke the few coarse hairs remaining upon his head.

During our hour together I relay stories of my children, trying to distract his mind from pain. I know he isn't really listening, but he politely lies there as the sole captured audience member. He drinks some water, throws up several times, and finally falls asleep before my mom returns home.

Driving the familiar country roads back to my house, the navy sky swallows me up. I turn off the radio, opting for the opportunity to communicate with my Heavenly Father instead of mindlessly tuning out.

At first, the words barely escape my dry mouth. But as I permit wet tears and emotions to surface and then overflow, the words do too.

"Please, please help him feel better," I meagerly beg.

The close-at-hand memory of him vomiting out the rejected medications resurfaces. I also hear him saying, "My chest is feeling less heavy." And I remember how his arms and legs calmed before he drifted off to sleep. The Holy Spirit is delivering the message that Heavenly Father already answered that prayer.

So with the curve of the back road, my prayer turns to, "Thank you. Thank you for helping."

I glance at the navy skies again, glittered with paint strokes of wispy cirrus clouds. Farms and plant nurseries stretch to the skyline. Telephone poles and picket fences outline the empty road. I feel so small and distant from my Heavenly Father. I try imagining Him on His glorious celestial throne trillions of miles away. Yes, the problems of every person in the world rest upon His shoulders, but amazingly He still listens and watches over silly little me.

"Thank you for seeing us and for looking down upon us."

My eyes look up again, and the radiant and seemingly all-knowing man in the moon meets my gaze.

"Thank you for looking down upon us," I repeat.

Then the Holy Spirit brings to remembrance a passage of scripture in 1 Nephi 11. In this chapter, the Spirit Himself speaks to Nephi, presenting him with a vision full of symbolism. In verses 16 and 17 it reads, "And he said unto me: Knowest thou the condescension of God? And I said unto him: I know that he loveth his children; nevertheless, I do not know the meaning of all things."

The Spirit showed Nephi a glorious vision of the Virgin Mary and of the Lamb of God. He also revealed symbols of Nephi's father's vision of the tree of life. Then the Spirit exclaimed, "Look and behold the condescension of God!" (1 Nephi 11:26). Note the exclamation point—that's a rarity in the scriptures, marking a momentous expression.

Nephi then foresees the Savior, angels ministering, miracles and healings, and the crucifixion.

I ask myself, "Am I getting it yet? Do I understand that word *condescension*?" Outside the Sunday School classroom, my knee-jerk definition of the word relates to condescending or patronizing behavior—like a disrespecting teenager who rolls the eyes and mocks in a depreciating tone. But the loving condescension from our Heavenly Father is obviously not that kind of disdainful behavior. The condescension from our Heavenly Father is the equivalent of a parent stooping down to see His child, and it's the kind of loving attention we crave as miserable mortals. We desperately need to know He still loves and watches us. We need His watchful eye in order to make it through this worldly maze of decisions. It reminds me of my own children's urgent and constant pleadings: "Look at me!" and "Watch this, Mom!" Apparently, children of God never grow out of that phase.

Taking it a step further, the condescension of Christ is fully displayed in the Son of God's descent to earth, assuming human circumstances and settings to perform the most incredible, all-encompassing act imaginable.

The man in the moon seems to grin down at me. I'm starting to understand. As I approach town, homes grow closer together like my spurts of spiritual impressions. Even hidden under a blanket of stars, I begin to comprehend the pattern. It all points to Christ, and it is all motivated by love. Do I know the meaning of all things? I'd have to chime in with Nephi on that one. No, and I can't see the spirituality in all things either—but it doesn't mean it's not there. I can see and feel His love—and that's what keeps me going.

"Keep looking down on me," I pray. "And I will keep looking up." I even pull over to the side of the road to write that one down in my trusty spiral notebook.

YOUR TURN!

The Spirit asked Nephi, "Knowest thou the condescension of God? And [Nephi] said unto him: I know that he loveth his children; nevertheless, I do not know the meaning of all things" (1 Nephi 11:16–17).

What do you know? Write down what you know about God and Christ and Their love for you. Remember, like Nephi, you don't need to know the meaning of all things, but consciously identifying spiritual things you do know shows Him you're looking up and makes it even clearer that He's looking down.

Have you ever watched someone drown? I haven't, but my friend Karrie Brester has. She watched her eight-month-old from the water's edge, in horror, as he thrashed about in a community pool. At first he flailed frantically, gasping and panicking, chest heaving, water deepening all around him. Then the water caved in over the tip of his head, and his body fell limp. His eyes stared straight ahead. He sank. He couldn't call out for help, and he couldn't cause a commotion. He just sank, and that's when he was actually drowning.

Karrie told me that she often flashes back to that memory during days when she's the one sinking toward the bottom of the pool—when the waters of grief, sorrow, and heartache deepen and overcome her.

Just a few years ago, Karrie watched her husband spend thirty-nine brutal and painful days in the ICU, dying a bit more with each sunset. During that time, he received a blessing of healing and she (and many others) prayed, fasted, and anticipated a miracle. Karrie says she fully believed he would be healed and return to her family. Instead, she watched him die and leave her a widow of three young boys in Highlands Ranch, Colorado. In that moment—that moment of knowing he was really gone from earth—the Holy Ghost took over. Looking back, she says she's in awe of how composed she was able to be because of the Comforter. She spoke at her husband's funeral with confidence in the plan of salvation. She held it together as her three boys sang "Families Can Be Together Forever." She focused on raising her children and figuring out how to become master of this new life.

But as time passed, as the adrenaline withered away and life was supposed to go on, Karrie discovered new stages of mourning. First she mourned for her boys, the fact that they would not have a father, and all that that meant. She mourned for each milestone they'd reach without him: the father-son campouts, learning to fish, being ordained to the priesthood, the missionary prep and pep talks. Then she entered a stage of mourning for herself and the life she originally planned. This is not the route she ever anticipated or wanted. She wanted to grow old with her sweetheart, to mother with a helpmeet, and to spend her golden years serving side-by-side with her companion.

In the belly of bereavement, Karrie became her drowning son. She says she couldn't flail or cause a commotion or call for help. All she could do was limply lie in the fetal position on the bathroom floor and cry.

Thankfully, Karrie's son did not drown unto death—and neither has she. For God sends life-guards. Rescuers. Mortal angels. Karrie has been lifted by living lifeguards in the form of friends, family members, and strangers. Choice souls have stood up as her advocate. They have identified her needs when she could not, they have created a commotion to draw in others, and they have extended floatation devices to keep her afloat. In turn, they became her saviors.

Karrie told me of how her heart swelled when the refrigerator repair guy heard her story and volunteered to serve as her unofficial handyman. Another time, a woman came to work on Karrie's blinds and then shared Karrie's story with her Presbyterian congregation and recruited members of that church to bring Karrie's family meals for four months.

Once an anonymous soul sponsored her sons' soccer season.

Karrie's rescuers and experiences exemplify the importance of remaining diligently watchful and active in service. It proves that we cannot wait for the drowning soul to call for help. Oftentimes, they simply can't. The most impactful saving graces—the buoys in bereavement—have come to Karrie in the form of people willing to spring into action without waiting to be asked. Karrie says these rescuing lifeguards empathetically feel the pain alongside her and say, "Hey, I'm bringing dinner at 5 o'clock. You can put it in the freezer or eat it." They ask, "What time do your kids go to bed? I'm coming tonight to help with the bedtime routine." When unsure of how to offer comfort, they say, "I love you"—which is so much more comforting than not saying anything.

It has been three years since Karrie's husband passed, but she honestly admits she's just now in the depths of grief. There is no standard timeline for mourning. That being said, Karrie knows she will survive the sorrow and hardships because of the living lifeguards surrounding her. She trusts in others' watchful eyes and saving hands, because they are an extension of Heavenly Father's eyes and loving hands.

During our last conversation, Karrie told me she realizes she can't do this on her own, and she's so thankful she doesn't have to. She says it will take a widespread community to raise her children and to keep her afloat, and she's overwhelmingly grateful for the community of lifeguarding angels heaven sends her way.

CHAPTER 15

Three Little Words

Anna didn't eat much lunch, and she picked and prodded over dinner, but in between meals she persistently requested snacks. Well, *requested* is much too pleasant of a word—begged, nagged, and whined is more like it. We nibbled on a routine mid-afternoon snack before the sheep poop incident, but apparently carrot sticks weren't exactly what she had in mind. "Beggars can't be choosers," I chided, as I have heard my father-in-law say so many times before.

Her relentless pleas picked up again, so I quoted our family's standard response: "The kitchen is closed." This bought me thirty seconds before she tirelessly continued.

"Mom, I'm soooo hungry," she whimpered, clutching her tummy and filling the air with another drawn-out groan of despair. "Can I have some food, *please?*"

I too groaned—though mentally contained it with some self-control. I decided to test a technique I'd recently read on a parenting site ("Child Nagging and Negotiating," Amy McCready, *Positive Parenting Solutions*, accessed February 25, 2014, www. positiveparentingsolutions.com/parenting/end-child-nagging-negotiating-with-just-three-simple-words). With it promising to end child nagging and negotiating and only requiring simple phrasing and consistency, I figured it was worth a shot.

I looked her in the eye and asked, "Anna, have you already asked for snacks?"

"Yes."

"Anna, have you already received an answer?"

"Yes."

Her guilty little pink lips crinkled upward in the corner as if she were contemplating crying and smiling simultaneously.

"You have asked, and you have been answered. The answer is not going to change," I reassured her. "If you ask again, I'll just say three words: asked and answered."

She "hmphed" with discouragement and then became uncharacteristically quiet. Without another nag or request, she bounced off to play. Hallelujah, it worked!

Now, in the eight o'clock hour, we gather in the girls' room for nightly family scripture study. The children smell and look like fresh-out-of-the-box porcelain dolls, with wet hair from their shower, teeth minty, and clean pajamas on. They snuggle between bed sheets and stuffed animals, and Eli tries his best to sit still on my lap. Alex kneels between the toddler beds and opens the Book of Mormon, which we recently began reading for our second time as a family. (It took us approximately three years to read it the first time as a family—but hey, line by line, verse by verse, chapter by chapter, right?)

After a few verses, we came to 1 Nephi 1:16: "And now I, Nephi, do not make a full account of the things which my father hath written, for he hath written many things which he saw in visions and in dreams; and he also hath written many things which he prophesied and spake unto his children, of which I shall not make a full account."

Referring to Lehi's visions, dreams, and writings, Avery astutely asks, "Where are they?" And though I feel exhausted and only want my children to begin their dreams, the Spirit nudges me alert, sharpens my mind, and brings my recent conversation with Anna, about pleading for food, to my remembrance.

I explain that Joseph Smith translated those writings with

his scribe Martin Harris. After working together for some time, they had written 116 pages of Lehi's words. Naturally, Martin wanted to show his wife, his family, and others the manuscript. So Martin asked Joseph, and Joseph then asked God. Heavenly Father's answer was no.

But Martin asked Joseph again, and I imagine it was a little stronger and more desperate this time. So in turn, Joseph asked Heavenly Father again. Heavenly Father repeated His answer—no. But Martin just couldn't give up; he begged Joseph to plead to the Lord once more. Joseph asked a third time, and this time Heavenly Father conceded. But sadly, after Martin showed his wife, his family, and some others the manuscript, a terrible thing happened: Martin couldn't find the 116 pages. He desperately searched everywhere he could think of, to no avail. I can't imagine exactly how much panic, sorrow, and regret Martin and Joseph felt, but I am betting their feelings were excruciating. And because of this situation, our Book of Mormon begins with the first book of Nephi, not the book of Lehi.

My girls sit wide-eyed, sucking the flavor from every word of the summarized story.

"Joseph asked and was answered, but he kept on asking. Anna, do you remember our talk today about being asked and answered?" I wonder out loud.

Anna solemnly nods, and both girls understand completely. The scriptures have the best examples—for children and parents alike. And though we're generations apart from those in the scriptures, we often stand in need of the same lessons.

I too am guilty of asking again, after already receiving an answer. When Alex and I graduated from college and moved back to Oregon to start the first "real" job, we were determined to pursue the American dream by purchasing our own home. We lived with my parents for a few months while we scoped the hot housing market and saved money. We enjoyed our time with my folks, and so did our firstborn, but we longed for a home sweet home of our own.

We found a quaint house with a cheery red door for sale by owner in an adjacent neighborhood; it was out of our price range, but we decided to write a low-ball offer. We felt so excited and hopeful, but it didn't go through. The answer was no. I remember praying to Heavenly Father, full of disappointment. Looking back, I see that we didn't stop to listen and accept His answer; we just kept asking for what we wanted. So the house hunt continued, and a month or so later we came upon a new construction site in a nearby town. This time we approached the seller more fervently and placed an offer for the full asking price. To our surprise, the answer from the seller (and Heavenly Father) was no again. We weren't sure how that could happen but decided it must not have been the right house for us. Our prayers for a house increased in urgency and we ran full-speed toward the next potential residence. On this third attempt, Heavenly Father conceded. We became owners of a beautiful newly constructed townhome—just one month before the nation's housing market crashed and burned. We're still paying the financial consequences of this decision.

Yet just as with Joseph and Martin's experience, the "learning opportunity" has strengthened our desire to cast aside our own wills and solidified our resolve to listen and obey Heavenly Father's will.

After Joseph's painful lesson, the Prophet said, "I made this my rule: When the Lord commands, do it" (Joseph Smith, *Teachings of Presidents of the Church: Joseph Smith* (Salt Lake City: The Church of Jesus Christ of Latter-day Saints, 2011), 160). And of that statement Elder Bruce A. Carlson said, "This should and can be our rule as well" ("When the Lord Commands," *Ensign*, May 2010, 39).

I love how Heavenly Father takes my life lessons in one hand and scripture lessons in the other and then ties them into a timely and perfectly personalized bow. He is all-knowing, all-loving, and always inspiring. His gentle but firm parenting solutions inspire me to be a better parent, a better daughter, and a better believer.

After the amens of family prayer, nightly bear hugs, and lullabies—oh, and after last drinks and final potty trips too—Alex slips into the girls' room for a short story, and I receive a moment to snatch my notepad and record another moment. I sketch a simple bow and write the three little words that pull together this spiritual lesson to my everyday, ordinary task of saying no to pleading children: *Asked and answered.*

May I do better and be better with accepting His answers from here on out.

YOUR TURN!

It seems like the decisions grow bigger, more frequent, and more consequential as years go by. That's why decision-making is an essential skill to learn and to teach our children. I often struggle with my decision-making, but I know I must separate my desires and His quiet answers. It's vital that I obey His actions straightway.

So, what decisions have you been pondering and praying about lately? Can you separate your asking from His answering? What could you do right away to more fully obey His answers? How has accepting answers blessed your life in the past? Think of a personal example of hearing His answers that you can share with your children. Allow your children opportunities to make decisions, and make it a point to gently guide them as they strive to learn this vital skill.

Housekeeping lacks perfection. Perching upon my crow's nest at the top of the stairs, I view the landmass below—and what a mass it is. At the end of the day, trails of shoes and accompanying dirt splatter beneath the front door, and forgotten board game pieces string along the hallway, leading to the haphazardly discarded toys and trinkets that coat the carpet in a thick plastic film. Sticky fingerprints decorate doors, careless crumbs sprinkle floors, and craft supplies have me begging, "No more!"

Housekeeping is a never-ending battle, one I will never win. No matter how thoroughly I sweep the floors, crumbs return; no matter how hard I scrub the sink, scum accumulates; and no matter how many times we sing the "clean up" song, toys seem magnetically pulled to the floor. What should I do? I consider my options: 1. Give up, surrender to the losing battle, and watch my home as it delights hoarding families of rats. 2. Continue the endless cleaning cycle and live in mostly sanitary conditions. I'll pick the latter.

I attempt the newly acquired tactic of "telling myself a story" by remembering a phrase coined by a woman in our congregation. One day she unexpectedly stopped by to witness our chaos. She took one look and sighed. I thought it was in disgust, but it turned out to be formed from admiration. "Your house feels so alive," she said. Then she told me how much she missed the liveliness of her home now that her teenagers had fled to college campuses. So tonight I take a mental panoramic picture, welcoming the aliveness—even the alive bubbling goo on the countertops. I try to see from a heightened perspective, acknowledging the kids' handiwork as proof of their presence. And if there's anything I've learned from my moments experiment, it's the proof of His presence in every space, every breath, and every vision of life.

I also glimpse divine details in this never-ending housekeeping marathon, like the many spiritual goals I will never achieve in this life. For example, I will never serve everyone I could and should, I will never fully understand the Atonement, and I will never reach perfection. So what should I do? I consider my options: 1. Give up and fall into dark and damning eternal consequences. 2. Continue fighting the losing battle, disinfecting bad habits and living as spiritually sanitary a life as possible. I'll pick the latter. I'll even try to feel as alive as possible throughout my impossible and unachievable pursuits.

"Please don't nag yourself with thoughts of failure. Do not set goals far beyond your capacity to achieve. Simply do what you can do, in the best way you know, and the Lord will accept of your effort," President Gordon B. Hinckley said ("Rise to the Stature of the Divine within You," *Ensign*, November 1989).

He also said, "Life is to be enjoyed, not just endured" ("Stand True and Faithful," *Ensign*, May 1996).

Plastic swords and other valiant forms of defense. At nighttime, my children wind up instead of down. It's rare that a little one curls up with a blanket and weighty eyelids in hopes of sweet dreams. The signs for sleep at my house include nonstop running up and down halls, slamming doors, flicking light switches on and off (and on and off again), and causing an inevitable injury. It's all fun and games until someone gets hurt, and once a child cries in pain, the big mama finally declares it bedtime (the highest level of difficulty and final round of the day).

For the past six months or so, Eli has been the most difficult to get to sleep. He repetitively screams, "I'm scared! I'm scared!" at high octaves, which leaves me feeling terrible for the little guy. (Perhaps he knows this? But he seems so sincere!) Each night, we reiterate the safety of our home, and he gets a special prayer by his crib to help him calm down. Tonight, the regular routine isn't cutting it—he's still scared and I'm spent. I call for reinforcement (so thankful for my hubby).

Alex asks Eli what is so scary, and Eli firmly replies, "Da bad guys." So Alex does what every parent doesn't do—he hands him a sword (a toy sword). A gold plastic sword, solidified and strengthened by duct tape around the hilt. Eli likes the idea and apparently feels prepared for what may come. He spoons the sword and reports that he's officially ready for bed. I shake my head and smile in amusement. Our little guy is literally sleeping on his sword (see Ether 15:20).

What faith my wee warrior has. He truly believes his weak weapon and nonexistent swordsmanship skills will protect him from "da bad guys." I can't help but think of David's faith as a child standing in front of the bellowing giant Goliath. I'm guessing David honed his sling skills prior to this face-to-face battle, but David's faith wasn't founded on the sling clutched in his hand, or in his good aim. David's faith was founded on the God of Abraham, Isaac, and Jacob. For "with God *nothing* shall be impossible" (Luke 1:37; emphasis added)—not slaying a giant, fighting against an evil one, or enduring temptations from the giant evil one.

It makes me want to grab my weapon of choice, be

it sling, plastic sword, keyboard, or voice. Sure, whatever I cling to will be pathetic and imperfect, but if I fight to defend my God, my God will be with me.

"There I will be also, for I will go before your face. I will be on your right hand and on your left, and my Spirit shall be in your hearts, and mine angels round about you, to bear you up" (D&C 84:88).

I am not alone in this fight—and neither are you.

CHAPTER 16

Balancing Work and Glory

9:00 p.m.

Anna tiptoes into our room, curls bobbing, dark lashes batting, and pale pink silk nightgown bouncing. Air escapes her pouting, pursed lips, striking a new pathetic pose with each whine. "I can't sleep. I don't know how. I just can't fall asleep."

Naturally, I want to shoo her directly toward the door. When the clock strikes 9:00 p.m., Mommy's patience and energy evaporates. Rolling my three little piggies in blankets is tricky enough, but getting them to stay put has become downright dreadful.

Thankfully, my hubby still has a few ounces of patience left.

"You can sleep," he assures her in his deep, gentle voice.

"No, no, I *really* can't," she assures him with conviction.

"Yes, you can."

"No, I can't!"

Oh boy, this isn't going well.

Then Alex smartly selects new reasoning words.

"Anna, you've fallen asleep every night of your life. You've fallen asleep every night for the past four years. You did it last night, and the night before that, and the night before that . . ." His soothing voice trails.

It's fascinating to watch logic formulate into perfect sense within her mind. Not a comeback peeps because she simply can't argue those facts. Blank faced, our mini-ballerina elevates to tippy-toes, performs a 180-degree twirl, and twinkles toward her bedroom—where I'm sure she lies in the darkness contemplating her next move.

Likewise, the Spirit communicates with me at the perfect level of intelligence for my spirit's maturity. I love how the Holy Ghost soothes my spirit, speaking quietly and gently as He reassuringly points out facts. He tells me when I should or shouldn't do something. He testifies of truth and denounces evil. There's no arguing with the Spirit—all I can do is decide my next move. I can ignore promptings, push them aside, forget them, or embrace them—it's up to me. So, after a day spilling over with divinely detailed **mom**ents, I think it's time to decide my next move.

My faithful and faith-filled notebook sits beside me, and I add a brief synopsis of the last five minutes under the title "Can't sleep? Decide your next move." Then I flip the crisp paper pages between my fingers. They smell sweet. Today's game of finding spiritual symbols and His insights has filled so many lines that awe tingles throughout my body. Little thoughts, routine tasks, common words, and small situations have blossomed into a bouquet of vibrant and fragrant spiritual lessons still lingering on the air and in my heart. What a gift from Heavenly Father!

Henry B. Eying spoke of the effects from preserving spiritual memories, and he too felt overwhelmed when reviewing God's hand in his life:

> More than gratitude began to grow in my heart. Testimony grew. I became ever more certain that our Heavenly Father hears and answers prayers. I felt more gratitude for the softening and refining that come because of the Atonement of the Savior Jesus Christ. And I grew more confident that the Holy Ghost can bring all things to our remembrance—even things we did not notice or pay attention to when they happened. . . .
>
> My point is to urge you to find ways to recognize and remember God's kindness. It will build our testimonies. ("O Remember, Remember," *Ensign*, November 2007, 67)

I wholeheartedly agree. I feel strong and firm, not just in my testimony but also as a mother about His work. I feel empowered and strengthened by the Lord. My home and heart seem more peaceful as my mind fills with His symbols and sight. "Our insights, our talents, our abilities are expanded because we receive strength and power from the Lord. His power is a fundamental component to establishing a home filled with peace" (Richard G. Scott, "For Peace at Home" *Ensign*, May 2013, 30).

His symbols and sight surely come accompanied with His power and His peace. I read over my notebook pages once more and even breathe in their unique "new paper" aroma. They are soul-ticklingly delicious to me. I just can't put them down. Now what should I do with this beautiful bouquet? Stick them in a vase and admire them on the kitchen table for a few days until they wilt? No, not this precious gift; I must keep the lessons alive by learning and living them. I must really inhale them, digest them—chew and stew; then go and do. It will require great work, but I'm sure it will reap rewards of great glory. "This is my work and my glory—to bring to pass the immortality and eternal life of man" (Moses 1:39).

On this night, Heavenly Father's mission statement feels relatable. My biggest hope and dream is an immortal and eternal family. And as I work toward that goal, I am getting drenched in both work and glory. Just think about it. Work? Oh yes, motherhood is work. Buckets brim with cleaning supplies, library books stack to the moon, hampers erupt with dirty clothes, and to-do lists constrict my breath like a boa. Yes, every hour testifies of how much work motherhood is. I'm constantly exhausted by the amount of energy expended for my growing family.

At the same time, motherhood is awesomely glorious. Nothing makes my heart soar and swell like the sounds of siblings whispering about secret service, the girly giggles and curtsies of princesses with parasols, or squishy hands squeezing mine. When their blue eyes sparkle in anticipation of being tickled, I could just burst. I love kissing the curve of my buddy boy's nose and the way he curls up in my arms, lays his head along my neck, and strokes my hair—pure bliss. When the whole family is together—whether snuggling up on a Sunday morning or getting dirty in the garden—that's the most glorious time of all.

Like with most everything in life, balance is crucial. I need work *and* glory. It's just like my growing list of temporal and spiritual symbols. There must be temporal situations to find spiritual symbolism in.

"Like two sides of a coin, the temporal and spiritual are inseparable," explained President Dieter F. Uchtdorf. "The Giver of all life has proclaimed, 'All things unto me are spiritual. . . .' This means to me that 'spiritual life is first of all a life. It is not merely something to be known and studied, it is to be lived'" ("Providing in the Lord's Way," *Ensign*, November 2011, 53).

Given my experiences today, I recognize that seeing spirituality is a life—a way of living life, not just a one-day experiment. I refuse to leave my interpretation of this mortal experience up to a coin toss; I want to see both sides of the coin, the divinity right along with the day-to-day. It will take time, concentration, and self-discipline to develop the talent of seeing the divine details and lessons in my daily life on a consistent basis. And it will take much-continued practice to engrave the talent into a habitual, instinctive thought process.

But if I don't work toward that goal, I'm back to the beginning—feeling buried in diaper duty instead of discovering Christ's spiritual treasures in my duties. The reason I lost sight of the spiritual significance of my role is because I lost sight—His sight. The personalized divine details and lessons were still there, just waiting for me to discover them. Unfortunately, I missed many opportunities to learn from them, to be comforted by them, and to be shaped by them, simply because I wasn't looking.

I was as stubborn as the children of Israel, who refused to look at the healing brass serpent. Recorded in Numbers 21, the Lord sends fiery serpents as a punishment to the children of Israel for their incessant complaining. Then after Moses prayed for the repentant people, the Lord instructs Moses on an easy antidote: a brass serpent attached to a pole (Numbers 21:7–9). Whosoever will look at the brass serpent will live—but even then, not everyone will look and live (Alma 33:19–20).

In hindsight, I see that I've been bitten with a bad attitude about my work and probably complained more than my fair share. What a shame. Now knowing the antidote, I resolve to repent, look, and live. It takes work to see glory, and I don't want to miss out on His intended glory by focusing solely on the work.

During Christ's earthly ministry, when He taught gospel principles with symbols and parables, not everyone saw the true meaning—many multitudes missed out. Even His disciples felt confused sometimes, at least until Christ revealed the symbols' relevance in quieter settings, away from questioning crowds.

"He explained that he used parables both to clarify truth and to keep it hidden. That is, to those who really desired to know it for the right reasons, the key to the symbol was given and they understood truth more clearly; but to others, for various reasons, the meaning of the symbol escaped them and they remained in darkness" (Lenet Hadley Read, "All Things Testify of Him: Understanding Symbolism in the Scriptures," *Ensign*, January 1981; see also Luke 8:9–10).

Whether I unearth and understand the divine details or not, they're there, like diamonds in the rough. Today I discovered a gamut of strategies for uncovering valuable spiritual gems in my daily life.

My notebook contains these must-haves for clearly seeing symbolic **mom**ents:

- Seek my own divine nature before seeking the divine around me.
- Keep trying, and view repetitive reruns as opportunities to discover and rediscover.
- Tell myself a story to replace initial judgments.
- Closing my eyes to the world opens my eyes to His lessons.
- Remember, He's cheering me on.
- Weed out sins and take baby steps in the right direction.
- *My* Holy Ghost will craft personalized and uniquely appropriate lessons for my intelligence and circumstances.
- Laugh and learn—simultaneously.
- Action is essential.

- Faith, hope, and charity can get me through any hour.
- Servants get served.
- I may not see spirituality in all things, but I can feel His love, and that's what matters most.
- Obey straightway.
- Balance my work and my glory.

Looking over the list, I can't help but send prayers of gratitude and praise to Heavenly Father. He truly is in the details of my life! I love how Christ constantly glorifies His Father during His mortal work, and I want to be more vocal in my praises to God as I see His hand in my life. Like Christ, I want to give God the glory in all my work too. If I do so, I think the work–glory equation will balance better. Then at the conclusion of each day and at the final hour of my probationary state, I hope to sincerely echo the words of work and glory that Christ spoke at the conclusion of His Intercessory prayer: "I have glorified thee on the earth: I have finished the work which thou gavest me to do" (John 17:4).

YOUR TURN!

In your notebook, create two columns, one labeled "work" and one labeled "glory." Brainstorm lists of your work and the glory you see in your day-to-day. Do you live with a work/glory balance? If not, what small adjustments can you make to live more equally distributed?

Also, commit to keeping your **mom**ent notebook for a specific period of time. May I suggest *much* longer than a single day? Think big—let's stretch our souls. In that commitment, include a designated day or time to review your lessons learned. As you begin to see more clearly and feel Him more deeply, share what you're learning with others.

CONCLUSION

THE AFTERMATH

S low down!"

I've heard those words from piano teachers, debate team judges, audience members, friends, family, and most frequently from my darling mother. My dad's racecar roots have rubbed off on me. But as I zoom full-throttle toward life's next goal or deadline, I tend to overlook life's delightful and divine details—and often miss the main point entirely! By consciously seeking symbols, I find myself naturally slowing down. My mind slows to a more harmonized state, my spirit feels more alert, and the division between this world and my Father's world feels sheerer.

Discovering the divine details is like wearing a fabulous pair of rose-colored glasses. I never want to take this view away! Everything appears much more cheery and meaningful with those glasses. Even debilitating trials appear more like a bright puzzle to put together, rather than dark torture to pull me apart.

Seeking His sight has become a bit of an obsession, because every insight is sustaining and sweet. Through personal experience and experimenting, I have found that it is true: all things testify of Him. And if all things testify of Him, so must I. I'd like to shout it from the rooftops: He lives! Jesus Christ is the Son of God, the Prince of Peace, our Redeemer and Savior, and the

Head of this Church. No matter who others say He is, the most important question to answer is who *you* say He is.

Christ Himself asked, "But whom say ye that I am?"

My answer follows Simon Peter's, when he enthusiastically declared, "Thou art the Christ, the Son of the living God" (Matthew 16:15–16).

The answer to the question "But whom say ye that I am?" should impact my every thought and deed. It makes all the difference in who I am and what life is about—because He is the difference. Of course, I slip up, I fall down, and I say something I shouldn't and fly to foul feelings or thoughts. But I can always return to Him. I can cry at His feet, apologize, and start anew. He makes the difference; He *is* the difference.

Recently, my little ones and I went to the Portland Temple Visitor's Center. A reverent hush fell upon me and my crew as we opened the door and saw a large statue of Christ, with arms extended, welcoming us. A senior missionary beckoned us closer to the Christ statue. We inched forward. The senior missionary told us we could even get close enough to touch Him. We did. Each child felt the nail prints in the statue's hands and feet. The senior missionary then asked if we wanted to hear His words, and we did. After the short audio recording, the senior missionary invited my little ones to give the statue of Jesus a hug. What a tender moment, as six small arms reached around their Savior (well, a statue of their Savior) to give Jesus a hug.

In the divine details of this scenario, I see this senior missionary as our Church and all of the support within (through scriptures, people, books, videos, and revelation) beckoning me to come closer to Christ. I can hear His words in the Bible and Book of Mormon and from prophets and apostles who speak for Him. In fact, I can feel the holes in our Savior's hands and feet symbolically as I remember and experience the Atonement in my life. And yes, I can even give Him a big hug. He loves me—and every soul who has ever lived—so much. I know He wants to hug us. He pleads with us to "be faithful and diligent in keeping the commandments of God, and I will encircle thee in the arms of my love" (D&C 6:20). His grace is always given; His arms are permanently extended, just like that statue. He constantly calls, "Come unto me" (Matthew 11:28). It's up to me to step close enough and to accept Him, His will, and His ways so that I can throw my arms around Him through obedience, discipleship, and gratitude.

I know this is truth, with every fiber of my being.

YOUR TURN!

Just as testimonies grow with the bearing of them, insights grow with the sharing of them. Talk about the divine details you discover, write them down, post them on social media sites. Share the goodness. Not only will your insights and faith bloom in the process, but others' might too.

Insightful Scriptures for Discovering Divine Details

The following scriptures are grouped into four categories to provide study topics and direction as we focus on seeing with spiritual eyes. While reading these scriptures with mortal eyes, let's keep our spiritual eyes and heart open. In the "Focused Findings" area, you can record promptings, ideas, or thoughts that come into focus in your mind and heart while pondering His words.

May we see as He: God's perfect sight

Since we want to pattern our sight after His, we must first learn how He sees and what He looks upon.

> "But behold, verily, verily, I say unto you that mine eyes are upon you. I am in your midst and ye cannot see me; but the day soon cometh that ye shall see me" (D&C 38:7–8).

> "For the Lord seeth not as man seeth; for man looketh on the outward appearance, but the Lord looketh on the heart" (1 Samuel 16:7).

> "And behold, all things have their likeness, and all things are created and made to bear record of me, both things which are temporal, and things which are spiritual" (Moses 6:63).

> "That which is spiritual being in the likeness of that which is temporal; and that which is temporal in the likeness of that which is spiritual" (D&C 77:2).

> "Wherefore, verily I say unto you that all things unto me are spiritual" (D&C 29:34).

> "All things denote there is a God" (Alma 30:44).

Focused findings:

CAN YOU SEE THAT? Adjusting our vision

Heavenly Father offers our mortal eyes scriptural instructions for how to see spiritually and how to improve our vision in the dark.

> "Trust in the Lord with all thine heart; and lean not unto thine own understanding. . . . Be not wise in thine own eyes" (Proverbs 3:5, 7).

> "Blessed are the eyes which see the things that ye see: for I tell you, that many prophets and kings have desired to see those things which ye see, and have not seen them; and to hear those things which ye hear, and have not heard them" (Luke 10:23–24).

> "For they will hear my voice, and shall see me, and shall not be asleep" (D&C 35:21).

> "Believe in God; believe that he is, and that he created all things, both in heaven and in earth; believe that he has all wisdom, and all power, both in heaven and in earth; believe that man doth not comprehend all the things which the Lord can comprehend" (Mosiah 4:9).

> "But there is a spirit in man: and the inspiration of the Almighty giveth them understanding" (Job 32:8).

> "Judge not according to the appearance, but judge righteous judgment" (John 7:24).

> "Remember the worth of souls is great in the sight of God" (D&C 18:10).

> "And the world seeth me no more; but ye see me" (John 14:19).

Focused findings:

I WAS BLIND AND NOW I SEE:
Examples of sight changes

Elevating our sight and perspective is a process every mortal seeks in order to live with Him again. Here are five scriptural accounts of impressive vision changes to get us thinking and seeing more clearly.

"And Jacob awaked out of his sleep, and he said, Surely the Lord is in this place; and I knew it not" (Genesis 28:16).

"And Ananias went his way, and entered into the house; and putting his hands on him said, Brother Saul, the Lord, even Jesus, that appeared unto thee in the way as thou camest, hath sent me, that thou mightest receive thy sight, and be filled with the Holy Ghost. And immediately there fell from his eyes as it had been scales: and he received sight forthwith, and arose, and was baptized" (Acts 9:17–18).

"And Jesus entered and passed through Jericho. And, behold, there was a man named Zacchaeus, which was the chief among the publicans, and he was rich. And he sought to see Jesus who he was; and could not for the press, because he was little of stature. And he ran before, and climbed up into a sycomore tree to see him: for he was to pass that way. And when Jesus came to the place, he looked up, and saw him, and said unto him, Zacchæus, make haste, and come down; for to day I must abide at thy house" (Luke 19:1–5).

"And it came to pass that Moses looked, and beheld the world upon which he was created; and Moses beheld the world and the ends thereof, and all the children of men which are, and which were created; of the same he greatly marveled and wondered. And the presence of God withdrew from Moses, that his glory was not upon Moses; and Moses was left unto himself. And as he was left unto himself, he fell unto the earth. And it came to pass that it was for the space of many hours before Moses did again receive his natural strength like unto man; and he said unto himself: Now, for this cause I know that man is nothing, which thing I never had supposed. But now mine own eyes have beheld God; but not my natural, but my spiritual eyes, for my natural eyes could not have beheld; for I should have withered and died in his presence; but his glory was upon me" (Moses 1:8–11).

"Then again called they the man that was blind, and said unto him, Give God the praise: we know that this man is a sinner. He answered and said, Whether he be a sinner or no, I know not: one thing I know, that, whereas I was blind, now I see. Then said they to him again, What did he to thee? how opened he thine eyes? He answered them, I have told you already, and ye did not hear: wherefore would ye hear it again? will ye also be his disciples?" (John 9:24–27).

Focused findings:

BELIEVING AND SEEING: Clear connections

The scriptures teach us that certain actions and concepts directly correlate with seeing spiritually. These principles go hand-in-hand with sight and can be studied and focused on individually or collectively.

"He who hath faith to see shall see" (D&C 42:49).

"Blessed are the pure in heart: for they shall see God" (Matthew 5:8).

"Handle me, and see" (Luke 24:39).

"And from henceforth ye know him, and have seen him" (John 14:7).

"O my son, do not let us be slothful because of the easiness of the way; for so was it with our fathers; for so was it prepared for them, that if they would look they might live; even so it is with us. The way is prepared, and if we will look we may live forever. And now, my son, see that ye take care of these sacred things, yea, see that ye look to God and live" (Alma 37:46–47).

"That which is of God is light; and he that receiveth light, and continueth in God, receiveth more light; and that light groweth brighter and brighter until the perfect day" (D&C 50:24).

Focused findings:

Cover art for *Everyday MOMents* was painted by Katie M. Berggren and represents the author, Jessica Poe, and her three children, as well as beautifully depicts meaning found in mothering. A wise willow tree stands as the backdrop to the little boy clutching a young tree sapling. This serves as an example of potential growth, both physically and spiritually. The mother looks heavenward while she encircles her children with love, protection, and guidance—as faithful mothers strive to do. All four faces appear peaceful, cheery, content, and close together, while their hair flows wildly in the wind. This exemplifies how the wild wind of the world can blow with great force, but when founded on faith in Christ, souls fill with an inner peace. That powerful inner peace provides eternal contentment and unity.

Katie M. Berggren, the mother of two growing boys, has been cited as the number one motherhood artist in America, and her artwork hangs in the homes of families in more than fifty-seven countries. Visit www.KmBerggren.com to view or purchase original paintings and archival prints, as well as to inquire about original, custom paintings.

About the Author

Jessica Poe is a mother of three and a collector of divine details. She's also a homeschooler by day and a writer by nap time. Jessica and her family live under the lively green trees of Oregon, where her heart flutters for bird-watching, berry-picking, and basking in small, natural moments.

Although she's a first-time novelist, Jessica has spent the last decade writing professionally for health-care systems across the nation. Prior to freelancing, she worked as a communications specialist for Intermountain Healthcare and earned a bachelor's degree in public relations from Brigham Young University.

Please visit www.jessica-poe.com to read more and share your own everyday *moments*.

0 26575 17741 1